"I found my Feats in These Sh[illegible]
strong call for us all to continue [illegible] giant steps toward who we want to be and what we want to do."

—James Reed,
bestselling author and Chairman of REED – Britain's biggest and best-known recruitment brand and the largest family-owned recruitment company in the world.

"The stories in 'My Feats in These Shoes' sparkle and shine with wit, warmth, and lessons for anyone looking for a place to not just fit in but stand out."

—Courtney Anderson
Founder/CEO SparklBands

"A delightful read, full of imagery and imagination, from a woman who knows how to step up!"

—Nanci Bell,
Author of "Visualizing and Verbalizing" and Founder of the global education firm, Lindamood-Bell Learning Processes

You will hop, skip, jump (and giggle) through this irrepressibly exuberant, poignant, and elevating romp!

—Paul G. Stoltz,
NY Times bestselling author and Founder and CEO of global research and consulting firm PEAK Learning, Inc.

"This book reminded me of the high heels and low flats I have worn and remember how humor, laughter, love and the right shoes are outstanding accessories in our lives."

—Heather Hutchens,
Vice-President, Strategic Planning at
John Paul Mitchell Systems

"I have watched her Ted Talks, read her books, and like so many of us, stood in similar shoes trying to gain my footing in life. A testament to life force, believing in yourself and taking giant steps, "My Feats in These Shoes" is indeed solely original."

—Helen Kirwan-Taylor,
Journalist, The Guardian, London, artist and speaker

MY FEATS IN THESE SHOES

My Feats in These Shoes

A solely original memoir
by

RONDA BEAMAN

BOOKS

Adelaide Books
New York / Lisbon
2021

MY FEATS IN THESE SHOES

A solely original memoir

By Ronda Beaman

Published by Adelaide Books, New York / Lisbon
adelaidebooks.org

Editor-in-Chief
Stevan V. Nikolic

For any information, please address Adelaide Books
at info@adelaidebooks.org

or write to:

Adelaide Books
244 Fifth Ave. Suite D27
New York, NY, 10001

ISBN: 978-1-955196-28-4

Printed in the United States of America

A portion of the proceeds from the sales of this book will go to Soles4Souls, a non-profit organization donating used shoes to change the world.

For the friends who have walked beside me,

for students who have kept me on my toes;

for my sons, daughters, and their children who

will follow in my footsteps,

and for Paul...finally, the perfect fit!

Contents

Never judge someone until you've walked a mile in his shoes. That way, when you do judge him, you're a mile away and you have his shoes.

—Emo Philips

Shoes are funny beasts. You think they're just clothes, but really, they're alive. They want things. Fancy ones with gems want to go to balls, big boots want to go to work, slippers want to dance. Or sleep. Shoes make the path you're on. Change your shoes, change the path.

—Catherynne M. Valente

Also by Ronda Beaman

You're Only Young Twice: 10 Do Overs To Reawaken Your Spirit

Student Development and College Teaching

Little Miss Merit Badge

Seal With a Kiss

Introduction

Shoes Speak Louder Than Words

A woman with good shoes is never ugly.

—Coco Chanel

"You have the ugliest feet I have ever seen. They are like little troll feet."

One barefoot summer afternoon when I was kid, I was sitting by our backyard pool chatting with my dad. We had just finished doing some laps, the Arizona sun was strong and un-relenting and our conversation was stilted and random. His sweet spots in conversation were sales and cars and sports, he was not especially adroit at connecting with a young daughter. I was riding this wave of his current attention and soaking up being seen not as one of his three kids, but as THE kid at that moment. I was hanging on every word, relishing his thoughts and opinions, holding on tight like someone would to a life preserver. Bobbing, rotating, and not wanting to let go of his generally stingy, but currently focused attention.

My legs were dangling back and forth from the webbed lawn chair as I tried to keep the so seldom from him and coveted from me conversation going. I asked about swimming strokes, hot dogs vs. bologna for lunch, and "how's work?" type stuff including:

"Daddy, do you like mustard or mayo on turkey sandwiches?"

"Daddy, do you like football or basketball best?"

"What is your favorite dinner that Mommy cooks?"

The questions were inane and not original, which also describes how I felt around my dad.

After my chirping asks and his one-word answers, he sighed and settled into silence, his dark glasses hiding his bright blue eyes. I hoped he was dozing off and not just bored. After a few moments, he turned his handsome face and shaded gaze to me and casually told me what he thought of my feet. The words, "You have the ugliest feet I have ever seen," sank my momentarily buoyant spirit. He continued,

"They are so skinny and bony, no one in our family has feet like yours. They're creepy."

He stood up, patted my head and strolled, like the good-looking boys I had seen at the high school pool stroll, slow and loose limbed, toward our swamp cooler, cooled house. He opened the sliding glass door, stepped inside and pulled the door closed behind him. I heard a click. He locked me out. In the closed glass door, I saw myself as a watery reflection, blurred and featureless.

I recalled another day by the same pool and hearing my dad tell my brother that his legs looked like pieces of dental floss hanging out of his underwear. I laughed, we all laughed, except my brother.

Well, she who laughs first....

I stood up, the flesh on the back of my legs dented with the pattern of the lawn chair and I looked down. Feet. I saw just feet. Two of them. Mine. My up 'til now sufficient and unconsidered feet. My heretofore fine feet that helped me run, jump, play tag, and walk to school five days a week. The very same feet at the bottom of the same legs I slapped while laughing when my dad made the remark about my brother's dental floss legs.

I lumbered over and sat down at the edge of the pool, dropped my bony feet into the water, splashed back and forth, and thought as deeply as an eight-year-old can about what my dad had said about my feet and why it made me feel like throwing up.

'Thank goodness it's not my face he thinks is ugly.'

Yet.

What would I do about that? What does anyone do about a face your dad says is ugly? I considered some of my friends and classmates and thought that their dads must have said something about the buck teeth, the crooked eyes, or the big nose. What did they do at a moment like that? Laugh? Cry? Ignore it? Accept it? I had no idea. It never once occurred to me that no one else had a dad who would criticize their child's face, or feet.

The idea that maybe most dads complimented whatever their child had going for them, like "You are so smart," or "Your pigtails are cute," really didn't cross my mind. The concept that a father could adore you from head to toe only happened in fairy tales. For all I knew, all parents found their children wanting or lacking in one way or another and today was the day I found out my deficiencies began from the bottom of my feet and had nowhere to go but up.

I pulled my creepy feet from the water, stood up, and walked toward the house. I looked back and saw wet, skinny footprints behind me. They were drying quickly on the pavement; disappearing like the footloose little girl I had been less than an hour ago.

The remainder of the afternoon was spent looking at my feet, examining and questioning what my dad had seen and wondering why I had missed the obvious deformity of what I had been standing on all these early years of my life. If I had missed my seemingly deformed peds, what else had I missed? What else was missing, ugly, or just not right? When would I hear about it? And what could I do about it?

Some kids build sandcastles, others play Barbie. My central preoccupation became my feet. I devised many a plan to prettify them, including using toe nail polish like my mother, using Coppertone Quick Tan on them so they weren't so ghostly pale, or desperately trying to pick up marbles with my toes to build some muscle on what, even I had to admit, were skinny and flat feet. I was frantic and obsessed in my pursuit of a positive and attractive way to walk in the world. And finally, one day I saw a sign. The sign I needed, pleaded, and prayed for—the sign that would lead me to my sole salvation.

It was on an easy three block walk—that I had made many times to buy cigarettes for my parents—in a gritty little strip mall that was home to a Circle K mini market and a barber shop, that I saw the 3D, weathered, and cracked black letters that read **Phil's Shoe Store**.

"Man Alive, Two for Five" waved a bright green and white banner flapping outside of Phil's, inviting any and all who entered to get two pairs of shoes for five bucks.

Whether sandals, slip-ons, sneakers, sling backs, high heels, pumps, flats, Mary Janes, or flip-flops, two pairs of shoes could be had at Phil's with a $5 bill. This wasn't just pay less, it was pay little and double your pleasure, double your fun!

Phil's was the palace where I believed I would find solace and sanctuary for the ugly stepsister feet I had been given. I could create my own fairy tale happy ending in a variety of straw, plastic, and patent leather slippers. Goodbye Ugly. So Long Skinny and Bony. Hello Stylish, Cute, or Sporty!

For many months—whether with birthday card money, babysitting jobs, allowance, or lemonade stand profits—I would stash the cash and hot foot it to Phil's Shoe Store and buy two pairs of pretty for my feet.

I could get the forest green loafers and the hot pink baby dolls, or the yellow t-straps and the rhinestone sandals. I loved Phil's Shoe Store and it became church in a box my size. I learned to worship walking in color, looking down to see the cute or stylish camouflage of my choice, and solving my own problems, footing my own bill.

I have come a long way since that summer afternoon with my dad. But, in so many ways, I am still that little girl stuck in the webbed lawn chair. My dad's words that day, and on so many others, are seared into my psyche and stuck—like the pattern of the plastic chair on the back of my legs.

Phil's Shoe Store and all the shoes to follow are surely stand-ins for how and why I cobbled my way to bigger strides than I might otherwise have taken. Perhaps if I had been treated like a princess by the first man I loved, I would have been secure and satisfied enough with my lot in life that I may never have tried to take giant steps or find my own glass slipper.

What follows are the stories of the different styles and sizes of shoes that took me into and out of tight spots. Shoes that I wore to step up or back. Shoes that helped me cross bridges and climb mountains—and accomplish some small, medium, and large feats.

Chapter One

Baby Needs New Shoes

It isn't the mountain to climb that wears you out,
it's the pebble in your shoes.

—Muhammad Ali

My dad's favorite books, *Mein Kampf, Think and Grow Rich,* and *How to Win Friends and Influence People* are book-ended by my bronzed baby shoes.

The shoes have deep copper colored wrinkles and folds, they cave in slightly at the arch, and one is missing a shoelace. My report cards aren't bronzed, neither are my pacifiers, baby blankets, rattles, or bottles. My graduation shoes or wedding shoes are not plastered for posterity, only my baby shoes.

No other personal artifact, it seems, is significant enough to be preserved for all time as what I had on my feet when taking my first steps into the world. I chose to believe my bronzed baby shoes are a tiny monument to potential and promise. Overcome by this notion, I once made the mistake of asking my dad who it was that had my shoes bronzed and he said, "Why would I know? What a waste of money…and copper."

Seeing my bronzed shoes on my parents' shelf as a young girl made me feel I might be destined for something momentous, despite my dad's snide comments or unsettling reading material. Looking at them made me feel a little famous; like, 'Why would my shoes be preserved for all time if I wasn't special? To someone?'

I considered the possible benefactors and did a mental lineup of possible characters who might have cared enough, or loved me enough to save the shoes, schlep them to the bronzing place, and ensure they were preserved for all time. The whole process took some effort—and as my dad had grumped—someone spent the cash. Both of which were in short supply when I was born.

My maternal grandmother, Echo Rose, stood 5'4" barefoot, was substantially redheaded with bright blue eyes, a DD chest, and the predictable man trouble that often accompanies those measurements. A photo of her at age seventeen shows her scowling into the sun, her arm raised and her hand above her forehead, but the sun still directly in her eyes. She is circled by a number of men from the 1932 Olympic track and field team. She had volunteered to be a times keeper at the prestigious event. None of the men were looking at the camera, their eyes were fixated on my grandmothers amply filled angora sweater. She looked not just aware but accustomed to the attention. In fact, decades later in her life I was with her when a man rushed to open a door for her.

"Grandma, you've still got it!" I joked.

"At this age, who needs it? she replied, not missing a beat.

The day I was born, she was thirty-six years old. Her own mother, my great-grandmother, had been forty when she started having children and then had eight of them in succession. Echo was in the middle of this pack and despite so many efforts, with so many men, in so many jobs, the middle is pretty much where she stayed throughout her life.

At the time of my birth, she was also a divorced, single, working mother of three children who still lived at home—one of them being my teenaged, pregnant mother. Echo had dreams and aspirations of her own but, not unlike her name, whatever she tried to be or do with her life came back to her a little less strong and clear than how it started. She wanted to be a good mother but married crummy men who didn't support her. She wanted to be a performer but instead loaded her daughters with lessons and costumes and hoped, in vain, they would become the star she wanted to be. She worked fifty hours or more a week as a WWII riveter, developed people skills in retail customer service, and eventually was promoted to a fashion buyer position at a large and prosperous department store long before it was chic to have a career.

Echo had an easy laugh, a love for life, and a poet's soul. She wrote poems about her day, poems about her family, her garden, and her work. She wrote poems she sent as birthday cards, poems for holiday gatherings, and metaphoric poems about sturgeons.

"*When does the sturgeon get the urgin?* It's in the spring."

"*When does the flower feel its powe*r? It's in the spring."

In all of the eighty-eight years I knew her, I never heard her say "I'm tired." Although in constant pain and taking daily morphine for a back injury, she never missed out on a chance to have fun. Her motto was, "I'm gonna feel awful sitting at home or going out— might as well go out!" And off she would go, me in tow, to Disneyland, museums, carnivals, or cake decorating class. She gave me a roof over my head, a crib in her room, and from the beginning made me feel like I was worthy of the "Sugar Plum" nickname she gave me. She taught me that a woman could call her own shots, build her own life, and have meaningful work outside the home long before society agreed. "Who needs a man?" she would always say, and then grab a hammer, a needle and thread, or a paycheck and get "it," whatever "it" was, done.

Where was my grandfather?

This question echoed many times a day from extended family, neighbors, my mother, my ten-year-old aunt and my seven-year-old uncle. I didn't miss him because I never saw him or even met him until I was in my thirties, and that turned out to be too soon.

At the time of my birth, he was a bellman at a tiny, exclusive hotel in Hollywood. That's not accurate. He was a tiny bellman, at an exclusive hotel. In pictures from this era, he is standing as tall as a guy 5'5" can stand and is wearing a jaunty pill box hat, tilted slightly to the right, a red vest, white shirt, slacks, and a pair of loafers. Loafer being a key descriptor of more than his shoes. When he didn't go to work, which was regularly, he played the ponies at Santa Anita racetrack. He left his hotel job early and often, caught a bus to the track, and lost any money he had made at his hour or two on the job. The only shoes my grandfather was ever interested in were his own or those worn by a horse.

My seventeen-year-old mother, Echo's eldest daughter, was also a petite redhead. She was often mistaken for Debbie Reynolds and just plain mistaken. For instance, the prom night I was conceived—an event that gives a whole new meaning to Senior Ball—she erroneously believed the boy in the backseat meant it when he said he loved her. By this time, she had been cooking, cleaning, ironing, sewing, and standing in for her working mother—and a father who never ponied up—and was itching to be in someone else's shoes.

My dad, the boy in the aforementioned back seat, was a handsome star athlete and smooth talker. He was popular, a "catch", and my mother willingly lost more than her Keds in the back seat of his Oldsmobile.

Nine months later I was born, but the childish things like the prom queen crown and letterman's sweater were never, ever, really put away. I grew up with the stories of the glory, glamour, and popularity my parents had reluctantly surrendered "because we had you."

Sometime after the ink had dried on my birth certificate footprint and before my first birthday, my dad moved into the very house my mother had tried to escape by dating him. And speaking of escapes, my dad had tried; leaving my mother to attend college in another state and even pledged a fraternity. Once I was born though, he was forced to pack up his university potential and pipe paraphernalia—a new habit he thought made him look collegiate—and return to the pledge he had made my mother.

My parents still had pimples, no paycheck, and delusional, somewhat unwarranted self-regard. I am sure there is a scientific or psychological name for this disorder. Throughout my life I just called the syndrome Mommy and Daddy.

My adolescent parents could barely take care of themselves, let alone another needy, self-centered, hungry human. With idle days at home they practiced creative child-care. One favorite activity became scooping me up out of my crib, standing me on the ground in front of them, and dropping ice cubes down the back of my diaper. Watching me stomp my pudgy, baby feet around the house gave them cheap laughs and me welts.

My teen parents were overwhelmed and under-prepared, maybe even uninterested, and if ice cubes down the pants were considered playtime then buying or preserving baby shoes were most likely not a priority.

And my gambling grandfather, with his losing track record, was most likely extremely careful to never utter, "Baby needs new shoes!" for fear he might have to provide them.

It does not take too many leaps of armchair psychology to know my first pair of shoes were purchased by the only employed and generous person in my family...my grandmother, Echo.

It makes me smile to imagine her making a special detour home from work to pick up the bronzed baby shoes she ordered. I like to think that she was looking at them and smiling while she recalled those moments when she held my hand and watched me walk—wobbly, then willfully forward, taking my first steps toward an unclaimed childhood.

Put Yourself in My Shoes
It's not where you've been.
It's where you're going.
RB

Your past doesn't define you.

Sure, my dad kicked my self-esteem to the curb when he told me my feet were ugly. Shame on him. But if I let that comment—or the other hundreds like it—define me forever, shame on me. And the same goes for you. Better to concentrate on who, what, and where you can find or create love than hold on to disappointment and despair.

You can blame parents, teachers, whoever and whatever for your depression, failures, anxiety, lack of focus, and ongoing heartache. Heck, blame someone else for every wrong, every slight, every set back you have faced. How's that been working for you so far? I'll answer that—all you're getting from the blame game is emotional bunions!

At some point, you have to put on your big boy or big girl boots and get on with it. The world doesn't care if you give up, if you stay standing in one place claiming everyone let you down and it's all their fault that you stepped in it. Nope, the world just keeps on going without you.

I have never known anyone great who didn't face hundreds of pebbles in their shoes as they climbed their mountain of purpose, contribution, and meaning. What do they do? They untie their shoes, pick out the biggest pebbles, throw them underfoot, put their shoes back on and then put all their weight into pulverizing the remaining gravel holding them back or down—and then they keep climbing.

Chapter Two

Blue Suede Slippers

A journey of a thousand miles begins
with a pair of fabulous shoes.

— Hudson and Bleecker

In an annual and painful rite of passage I am being dragged by my sweater sleeve and mother toward certain doom.

Today is shopping for school shoes day, at JCPenney's. This is always depressing and an affront to the fashion forward girl I believe myself to be. Depressing because price, not style rules the day and an affront because cheap shoes are always black or brown when I am definitely a red or hot pink kinda girl.

My mother, as seemingly eager to get this over with as I am, begins to turn each ugly black or brown pleather shoe over to check prices pasted on the bottom of the thin and gummy rubber soles.

She finds a dull black clodhopper that resembles shoes I have seen farmers wear in our Encyclopedia Britannica illustrations of the Dust Bowl. She raises a particularly odious oxford, turns it slowly to the right, then back to the left, pointing at it with her index finger, her smile forced and menacing as she displays a female version of a grandpa shoe like a valued prize on a game show.

'All this and shoelaces, too!' says the imaginary host my mother wants me to hear.

"You might not like these shoes when you look down at them while wearing them. But everything looks bad from an elevated angle. Remember how ugly and dull Phoenix looks when you see it from an airplane? But from my angle they are cute and my angle is what everyone else's angle is anyway." She smiles and winks my way. Winks! My mother has said repeatedly that she is no good at arithmetic, and this talk of angles confirms it. 'Phoenix looks bleak from an airplane window because it is.' I think. All of us involved in this adaptation of turning a sow's ear into silk routine—my mother, the clammy salesman whose name tag reads Gordy, and probably Mr. Penney himself—know these shoes are only included in the fall lineup because of the price and from any angle, from close up or miles high, the shoes are horrible. A cheap, barely better than barefoot, insult to foot and eye. I imagine the pitying look of a teacher who will, upon seeing me in these school shoes, invite me to sit close to her desk so I don't have to walk so far if I need her help. These shoes scream orphan, limp, brace, or cane.

I divert my eyes from the black shoes being favored by my mother and do my own furtive glance slowly to the right and then to the left and see all the shoes I will never get to try on, buy, or wear because they cost too much, are too impractical, or are simply not in the hunchback line my mother and her singular angle prefer.

And then fate steps in.

A design of furry, wispy, and baby blue jumps out at me and holds my gaze, mesmerizing and hypnotizing me as I walk slowly toward the glittering vision on the glass shelf. I stand before an art piece slipper, incandescent and breathtaking. The Penney's shoe department is fading into the background along with my mother and Gordy. Like a shoe horse with blinders, I can only see what is directly in front of me. Seemingly surrounded by colorful rings, like the planet Saturn, the object of my desire is otherworldly and certainly not seen or worn by anybody in my suburban solar system. My ears are ringing with a choir singing hallelujah. I levitate to the top shelf, third row over, and reach for this blue confection. It is feminine, soft, plush, and has a tiny lifted heel of suede. Doris Day wears slippers like these, boys like Fabian, or Moon Doggie or all of the Beatles fall in love with girls who wear slippers like these.

Why can't I be one of the girls who wears slippers like these?

My daydream is disrupted when I hear my mother asking Gordy the salesman for a pair of those sensible black grave digger shoes in my size.

I float over to both of them, holding the prized slipper and ask, for fun, just for fun, to try on the slippers. I don't really ask, I beg. I beg to try on the slippers. "Please," I grovel…"let me just try them on…without my white socks."

Mother nods her head twice and says, "If it means that much to you, knock yourself out." I hear nothing after the nod of approval. Her lips are moving and now so am I, as fast as I can, pulling my old shoes and white cotton socks off my feet, tossing them with the ready disregard and disdain I have for them.

I will never know why my mother agreed to my pleas and please. Weariness? Heat stroke? Possibly remembering when she also wished for beauty and pizazz? Or, simply to get me off her back? Whatever prompted her out-of-character agreement, I will never know. I never asked, afraid that the reason may not be as loving as I wanted it to be, afraid she would not even remember, and of course, why should she? This was my shoe show, not hers.

Gordy returns with two boxes. I dutifully try on the black school shoes. I have seen pictures in the newspaper of Israel's Prime Minister Golda Meir, and these are exactly the shoes she wears. I do not want to lead a country; I just want shoes to help me leave Phoenix.

But I remain calm. I smile innocently at my mother and then a smile for sweet, helpful Gordy. I take my time. I do not want to appear desperate or unstable. I want to be worthy and charming, like someone born to wear beautiful shoes.

"May I try on the slippers now Gordy, my good man?" I ask. I had heard the butler Mr. French on the TV show, *Family Affair* called "my good man" and this seemed like the appropriate moment to pull this phrase out to increase my chance of being seen as a sophisticate.

The black shoes were boxed in cardboard and stuffed with more cardboard. Bleh. The blue slippers are wrapped, *wrapped!* in bright pink tissue. They sound elegant and enticing as the tissue unfolds with a sighing sound, or maybe that's me? No, I am not sighing, I am panting and starting to sweat ever so slightly. Less than Gordy, but still. The slippers are unwrapped and are finally presented to me like a princess, my new best friend Gordy bowing down ever so slightly. Slowly, silently I slide my bony, skinny right foot into the silky, soft, gossamer wedge and the transformation is instantaneous. My foot has never looked like this, translucent and ladylike. It's like my foot has no other option than to point. The slipper is pure glamor and with them on my feet I, too, become glamorous.

The feathers run horizontally across the top of my foot and as I stand, they sway slightly side to side, the way the coral on a reef does when a wave washes over it. In fact, the slipper is the color of the ocean and makes me feel like I am walking on water. Or air. Or anywhere besides the JCPenney's shoe store at the Chris-Town Mall in Phoenix.

I walk toward the mirror regally and give myself the once over.

From my plaid shorts up past my popsicle smudged t-shirt and finishing at my Toni over-permed hair I am just a regular, albeit scruffy, kid. However, from my ankles to my toes I am a goddess. I want all of me to be like my feet. To be elegant. To be special. To be chosen and favored.

I attempt to strike a deal with my mother. I beg and plead. I promise I will wear the black oxfords all year, I will make them last, I will never ask for a new pair and I will never complain or use words like ugly, awful, or hideous when I put them on, nor pout or plead or even mention needing new shoes if I can only, please, have the blue slippers too. If I don't need another pair of school shoes this whole year, she still comes out ahead on expense, I tell her. This is a good deal, I argue.

My mother continues to surprise me by agreeing to this deal. She must have been motivated by imagining a year of no complaining about my ugly school shoes. I am excited and blithely ignorant to the scope of the deal I just tied up.

Both pairs of shoes are mine. For better or for worse, until next year do us part.

Through wind, rain, sleet, snow, during recess, Sunday school, softball, and Saturdays I wear the black clodhoppers. They begin to fall apart by mid-December. They have Elmer's Glue holding the soles on by February and by the last week of school in June, I might as well have been barefoot.

But I really didn't care. Much.

I began to care a bit when classmates made fun of the sound my flapping soles made as I walked from my desk to the pencil sharpener. I cared a bit when my teacher asked if my daddy lost his job and to let her know if things were OK at home. But all in all, the humiliation and teasing, the unsupported arches and heel blisters were a minor price to pay for the way those slippers made me feel when I got home and traded up from black to blue.

I was only a girl when I chose the blue slippers knowing it would cost me ugly all day, all year. I didn't listen to my mother or to the shoe salesman, I cared not a whit about what others would think, and instead was overcome by some inner essence crying out for beauty no matter the beastly cost. Thanks to the blue suede slippers, I learned early that life is a series of big and little trade-offs, of sacrifices, and consequences; but it's worth whatever it cost you if the shoe fits who you want to become.

Did you know that sea urchins have no eyes? Everything they see, they see through their tube-like feet. They sense beauty. They touch threat or danger. They handle purpose. They feel with their feet what matters to them for surviving and thriving. Like an urchin, we can feel our way to beauty and grab what we need in order to possess a small amount of specialness. Whether it's something you wear on your feet or finger, perhaps a dollop on your taste buds, regardless if it's in your head, or on your heart—choose what lightens and brightens your walk through the world.

I think we often get too consumed in choosing what's practical, in listening to others help us define ourselves, in doing what we think is right. We all feel the need to be rational, logical, and sensible with our purchases, our food choices, our dating life, and our shoes. But sometimes what's the harm in saying, "I just want to do this, or have this, or buy this, and I don't even know why."?

Maybe your brain, or your mom, or your boss doesn't actually know what you need. Maybe your heart has all the answers. Maybe you shouldn't think about it so much and just be. Just act. And, like the sea urchin, just feel. You might find yourself a better partner, job, or place to live. Or a really cute pair of kicks!

Chapter Three

I Can't Tap Dance in Tennis Shoes

Listen to my feet and I will tell you the story of my life.

—John Bubbles,
originator of Rhythm Tap

I may have been a little elf, but I had big dreams.

I continued to believe, despite mounting evidence to the contrary, that I was a big talent stuck in a little body and surrounded by small thinkers. I had a song in my heart, which is where my dad said it should stay. My only hope, therefore, for being discovered as the next Mouseketeer Annette or Beach Babe Gidget was to find a receptive audience with sophisticated tastes beyond my home and the narrow-minded critics within it.

It's not that I hadn't tried and tried to get parental funding for piano lessons, voice lessons, any lessons, but the answer from my dad was always a swift and consistent no.

"You don't need lessons, you need gumption. Quit wasting your time bugging me and just stand out on the corner and start singing."

Busking on a corner was much more preferable to his standard recommendation, "Go play on the freeway."

Home was a tough crowd. If I could make it there, I'd make it anywhere.

School became the perfect anywhere. There was a captive audience when I answered a question or gave a book report. I could rehearse (my preferred term for studying) and get good reviews from teachers. In addition, there were opportunities to star in pageants, plays, skits, and sports. To top it all off, the venue for my earnest—some, like my family, might call—overwrought, performances changed on a regular basis because we moved at least twice a year. School for me was a continuing gig and constant road show.

By fourth grade I had been the new student at eight different elementary schools in eight different neighborhoods. My family moved as a hobby or a habit, I am not sure which. My parents rented single level ranch houses we were never actually in long enough to call home. The decision of where to live was based on the cost of the rent, not whether we remained in the same school district or postal code. It was never clear to me why these ramshackle places were called ranch houses. Not a horse, cow, saddle, or wagon to be found. We would unpack, locate the local pack of cigarettes and loaf of bread market, usually a 7-Eleven convenience store, eat a few home cooked meals, meet a neighbor or two and then onto the next ranch, partner.

I exploited being the new kid at school as an opportunity to try on various personalities, hairstyles, and accents, and even names. At one school I might be Roni, at another I would use my middle name, Ann. I developed additional acting, singing, or dancing skills by auditioning for everything and joining any club or team that would have me. In this way I became well versed in disparate skills like chess, tennis, swim team, and judo.

I felt like I was building a set of skills that would serve me well as a movie star. Think of it—and I did think of it all the time—I wouldn't need a stunt double because I would know how to do whatever the role needed me to do. Jump from the roof of a house? Check. Swim across a raging river? Check. Impress a Hollywood agent…gonna Check, someday.

Each move brought varied experiences for my show biz resume. I dabbled in scriptwriting and character development by a) determining which character I wanted to be in any given day, week, month, or school and b) what script and lines I needed in order to be accepting, interesting, or popular. It was exhausting and exhilarating at the same time. For example, at one school I might be the girl who was on Mickey Mouse Club as an alternate.

"Oh, you didn't see me? Must not have been the month I was on," then, poof, we had to move before anyone realized I was making it up.

At another, I was the girl who had won the talent show at the state fair.

"Oh, it wasn't the Arizona State Fair, this was when I lived in Oregon."

Like any good grifter, I mean, gifted storyteller, by the time the other kids got wise, I had moved on. New school, new story.

And so it was that on one of these occasions, at one of these schools, when a teacher asked, "Who here has taken at least two years of tap dance class?" I hoisted my hand fast, first and furiously.

It must be patently clear by now that I was not a hoofer, especially a trained one, but I had been creatively faking it till I was making it so often that I believed my own praise filled press…mostly because I wrote it.

The teacher picked me and seven other girls with equal hand waving prowess and asked us to assemble in the cafeteria after school for our first "run through," which I thought meant we were going to "run through" the cafeteria. 'Piece of cake,' I thought. I scanned the classroom and did a quick once over of the other seven girls. They were of various size and shape, ponytails and pageboys, braces and eyeglasses. I smugly believed, lessons or no lessons, if they could dance, I could dance.

That afternoon seemed to be one of the longest of my school life as I waited and waited for my dance debut. I was more than ready for my star turn and confident I could dance like Shirley MacLaine; whom my dad called 'pug-ugly' yet was the star of the movie musical *Sweet Charity*. I was jazzed and ready to dance, show my stuff, reveal my talent.

At the long-awaited hour, once gathered in the lunchroom, the teacher asked us to think of her not as a teacher, but as our choreographer. 'Show biz types change identities as often as I do,' I thought, seized with a warm kinship for my choreographer that I did not feel for her in her day job as my teacher.

We were lined up from short to tall, with me as elf #3 and readied to do a run-through. It was interesting to me that the lunch tables were still in place, making a real run through the cafeteria a bit more like an obstacle course.

'Ah, she must want to see if we are nimble,' I thought.

"Alright, ladies, I just want to see how you move," she said, "please each of you start out with a walking cramp roll."

'Cramp roll?' I was puzzled. 'No run through? Cramp roll sounds painful. I panicked and began to improvise the Stop, Drop, and Roll I learned in my Girl Scout Safety Course. I stopped at Stop when I realized the girls on either side of me were standing upright and were simply flapping their feet. Flap-Flap right foot then more Flapping left foot. The dance line resembled the baby ducks I had seen splatting though the mud at the local hangout, Saguaro Park. No music, no timing, no

Fred or Ginger, just girls who looked like they were trying to remove dirt clods from the bottom of their shoes. This herky-jerky foot flinging was, evidently, the cramp roll. I cramped away and added a flourish here and there.

"Lovely!" our choreographer beamed, as she walked in front of and then behind the line up of dancing mudslingers, nodding what seemed to be approval.

'Now that our teacher is our choreographer,' I thought, 'her expectations of us have become substantially lower.'

If the flailing and flinging going on around me was judged lovely and the result of two years of study, I had to agree with my dad's decision to not invest in any lessons for me.

"Give me a Flap, Heel, Turn," she shouted.

Again, I took my cue from the girls on either side of me, who simply did the duck splat from before, then went back on their heel and turned around. Not an intricate, or as far as I could tell, graceful move.

I had plenty of practice doing what I was told at home and I was getting the idea that Tap was simply another form of "When I say jump, you ask how high." I was flapping and shuffling as fast as I could and more than ready for our break when the teacher, I mean choreographer, called out, "Shirley Temple."

'We get drinks!' I assumed. 'I could get used to this star treatment.'

Wrong again. This time the girls were all arms and legs, tennis shoe tapping their hearts out…so I joined in with a big smile on my face and a pert tilt to my head.

"Oh, THAT Shirley Temple!" I thought as I joined in the frenzy.

I'd seen enough of Miss Temple's curly crowned moppet's movies to know I needed to be ten percent dancer, ten percent dimples, and eighty percent personality. I moved both feet like

Fred Flintstone in his footmobile, in other words—as fast as I could while crossing my hands back and forth in front of me. A little shuffle off to Buffalo here, a kick or two there, jump forward and land on one knee, arms stretched wide and open.

Ta-da!

I hadn't noticed that the other girls were not Shirley Templing, and instead were standing in what I took as stunned envy and amazement as I channeled Miss Temple's electrifying performance in "Wee Willie Winkie."

Even the teacher/choreographer was momentarily speechless before announcing, "Ronda will be our lead elf, the rest of you will form a V behind her as the chorus line."

Lead Elf? This is what I had been preparing myself for my whole life, this was the part I was born to play, my first big break.

Today, Orangewood Elementary School. Tomorrow, Broadway.

I was elfin ready. My ears naturally stuck out far enough from my head that my dad called me a human trophy cup. I was small, I looked good in red...I only needed one thing...tap shoes.

I Flap-Heel-Turned my way home that afternoon practicing not just my steps but a step-by-step plan to convince my parents that tap shoes would be an investment in their future. Once a star, I would take care of them, let them enjoy the high life only I could provide. We would sit around my penthouse in Manhattan someday, sipping champagne and chuckling about how my fame and fortune began when they bought me a pair of tap shoes.

By dinner time that evening I had deluded myself into believing they would be excited for me, and for them. World famous daughters are hard to come by, after all. For the measly price of tap shoes, the world could be their oyster that I shucked.

Dinners at our house were formal, as in no t-shirts, no bottles or jars on the table, my dad still in his suit, and my mother in a dress and fresh makeup. It was as if they expected a camera crew to arrive any moment and film a new family comedy, *Leave It to Beaman*.

The conversation was choreographed by my dad and served with sarcasm and scathing personal criticisms about us, other people, and basically all residents of earth. Nightly topics might include droll observations like women should not be allowed to be newscasters, my brother is a pinhead, tuna casserole is a covert assault to him as a provider, most people are morons, how could anyone not think Jill St. John is a rare talent and the Joads from *The Grapes of Wrath* were victims of stupidity, not a dust bowl.

I wasn't really listening to his talk of the town on my tap shoe night, I was waiting my turn and rehearsing my lines, considering opening with, "How much money do you think Shirley MacLaine makes as an actress and dancer?" or maybe "I saw Juliet Prowse has a new house in Bel Air."

"Just think of it, so much money for dancing," I would add, convinced that appealing to greed and avarice always works, as that exact topic had once been a particularly enlightening dinner discussion my dad led.

As it happened, when there was a pause I panicked and rushed my argument, going straight for the jocular.

"Guess what? I was chosen as lead elf today!" I raised both my hands in a V above my head and did my best impish grin.

My mother asked me where this happened, as if she might be concerned my explanation would involve a van in the school parking lot and a man dressed in a clown costume.

"At school, in my class. My teacher is going to be choreographer for the holiday pageant, and she picked me! I am going to be in front, the lead dancer of all the other elves."

"Close to the edge of the stage?" Now my dad joined in.

"What? I don't know, we haven't been on the stage yet, just the floor of the cafeteria."

"Think about this, they probably put you in front because you are the shortest and that way the audience can see the other real dancers. And if anyone falls off stage, it will be the most expendable elf, the short one who can't dance."

Undaunted by this blatant attempt to derail me I kept my goal in mind, breezed past the unflattering comment, and pressed on.

"Daddy, this is a perfect way to get me off your back about lessons. I am going to finally dance. I don't need lessons. I am saving you money."

"Wrong. I wasn't spending money on dance class in the first place, so this isn't saving me anything. In fact, I bet you have to pay them for a costume for this so-called honor."

It was time to go for broke, get to the ask, seal the deal.

"I don't know about a costume, but I do need tap shoes." I said. "I can't tap dance in tennis shoes."

Him, silence.

Me, holding my breath.

The fact that he was thinking and not automatically saying no made me hopeful. I sat still as a stone watching him chew, chew, chewing oh so slowly, gazing straight ahead or maybe at the other end of the table at mother. I hoped he was imagining me in a sequined costume and top hat, tap dancing myself into the hearts of millions on my own weekly variety show. At last, he picked up his iced tea glass, took a sip from it, and put it back down. He dabbed his napkin lightly over his mouth, put it back in his lap, and turned to look directly at me.

Sitting on the edge of my seat, I was beginning to pant like a dog at the shelter who locks eyes with you as you approach his pen, willing you with all his canine cuteness to choose him and give him a home. I was on the verge of hyperventilating, each heartbeat pounding in my ears rang with the belief he would admire my pluck, consider my argument, and grant me this wish. I almost yelled, 'Thank you, Daddy' before he even spoke.

"Tap shoes? For one shot as the puniest elf? Nope. You have two options, nail something tappy to the bottom of a pair of your old shoes or borrow a pair of taps from one of your chubby pals who also think they can dance."

Many topics at our dinner discussions were intended for debate or debacle, but I could tell this was not one of them. He wasn't joking, he wasn't parrying for sport; he meant no. Not happening. Not up for discussion or argument.

That night, as I laid me down to sleep, I wrote my destined to be delivered Miss America, or Oscar, or Tony award winning speech.

"Thank you, America or the Academy, or the voting members and thank you to the teachers and friends who encouraged and recognized my enormous talent and assisted me on my road to great personal success, wealth, beauty, happiness, and fulfillment. And to the kids out there who have the same dreams, you can do it even if your dad won't buy you tap shoes and spends money on scotch and cigarettes instead of dance lessons for you."

The next day at school I did indeed ask one of the chubby tap dancers in the lineup if I could borrow a spare or old pair of tap shoes. I told her that mine were still packed in a moving box and I wasn't sure I could get to them before the rehearsals and show. Fortunately for me, she was nicer about helping me than my dad and lent me her old tap shoes.

The Holiday Pageant at Orangewood Elementary was SRO. Parents, grandparents, brothers and sisters, all jammed into the stuffy cafeteria which still had the faint smell of the beanie weenies from lunch that day.

My dance debut to the tune of "Frosty the Snowman" was a big hit, literally. Frosty, a clumsy boy stuffed into a three-hula hooped contraption covered with a white sheet, bumped right into me and knocked me flat on the floor. I did not, however, fall off the stage as my dad predicted, or hoped. I got back up, danced some more circles around the snowman and ended with a flourish of shuffles stage left. I searched from the wings for my family, who immediately left, so they missed hearing what I considered thunderous applause that greeted me at the curtain call.

I never returned the tap shoes I borrowed. And I never threw them away. I keep them as a reminder that lack of shoes, or lessons, or a roadblock who happens to be your parent were just the beginning of the obstacles ahead of me. I had to believe with all my heart it wasn't the person lucky enough to own tap shoes, or the one with the best education, best lessons, best parents, most talent or opportunity who would get what they wanted from life. It was going to be the girl, or elf, who got right back up when the anything, or anyone, knocked her down.

It's hard when no one believes in you or shares your vision for what you could or want to be. But it's absolutely deadly if you don't believe in your promise, possibility, or potential. Trust me, if you don't believe in you then no one else will. If you look in the mirror and think you will never be great, then you will never be great.

One of the methods for teaching dance is to put the steps you are supposed to take in sequence—mapping the footprints and placement of the right foot, left foot—with decals of feet to make sure you put your foot where it is supposed to be. If you make a misstep, or add an extra step, ball, change, if you don't follow along foot by foot, according to the pattern on the floor, you are dancing the wrong way. Life isn't like dancing class. Comparing your journey to someone else's or trying to follow in their footsteps to get where they got, only to fail, is discouraging, to say the least, and leads to giving up, at the most. It is better to do your dance imperfectly than to do someone else's dance perfectly.

You are on your own path. This means that even if you copy every step that someone else took to get somewhere—in life, a job, a love, an elf chorus line—your results will never replicate theirs'. Whether push or shove, your life is dictated by the steps you take, not the steps someone else took before you. Don't become a follower, take the lead and map your own singular and extraordinary steps. And when you stumble, just make it part of your inimitable dance.

Chapter Four

Size Five Mary Janes in Magenta

Step out of the history that is holding you back. Step into the new story you are willing to create.

—Oprah Winfrey

I had a model grandmother.

She didn't bake, or sew, I never saw her vacuum or scrub a sink. My grandfather brought her breakfast and a cup of freshly brewed coffee to her in bed every morning of their married life. I surmised that being beautiful often exempts you from the daily grind.

Once out of bed, usually after 10am, she was a tall, elegant, blue eyed, ivory complexioned fashion model for high end department stores throughout Portland, Oregon.

In contrast to my mother's mother, who loved to concoct marzipan wonders for birthday cakes and handmade our matching skirts and shirts at Easter, my father's mother had custom tailored clothes, belonged to a country club, and had a cocktail before dinner. Generally, it was a gin and tonic accompanied with a swizzle stick which she swizzled with her pinkie lifted high above her remaining, stirring fingers. Although she was from a family of farmers in Kansas, her elocution was nuanced, rehearsed, and "veddy" British sounding. She only broke into a mid-western twang when she had two or more of the swizzled drinks.

She had doted on my dad, her only child, making him her preoccupation when not modeling. That profusion of attention may be the reason there was no doting going on for anyone in our house. Maybe she set the bar too high and he knew he couldn't compete? Or was it too much of a good thing, perhaps? Most likely, he felt he was worth the dote and we were not.

I asked him once why he didn't have brothers or sisters, and why, oh why, I had both and he said, "When you reach perfection, like my mother did, you stop. In your case, we had to try two more times."

One of my major lucky breaks in life was being chosen to spend a few summers with this grandmother, Meme, and grandfather Daddy Bob, by myself, sibling free, with them in loco parentis. My grandparents had volunteered to babysit me once I was potty trained to give my teenaged parents a chance to patch together adulthood. The fact that I was named after their dearly beloved son Ronald made me their favorite, and I always felt it, knew it, and treasured it. Meme and Daddy Bob, names I gave them when I started to speak, were pretty chafed with Ronald when he got my mother pregnant but being a happy baby—a baby who actually cooed, burbled, and smiled—almost upon first breath, made me irresistible. To them at least. After all, the only other baby they had really known was my dad and they found me to be the perfect follow up.

Meme would take me to luncheons at restaurants festooned with crystal glasses and cloth napkins, as well as afternoon teas served by men in red and gold jackets who poured mint tea into fine bone china cups and called me "Miss." We attended modeling shows at swanky stores filled with well-heeled and well-dressed people. We strolled through museums to study art, perspective, color, and theme. My hair was cut by stylists, not beauticians, none of whom wore a plastic apron. We sat in velvet seats for weekday matinees. Daddy Bob took us to the live theatre, the Aqua Follies, sailing on friends' yachts down the Columbia River, and dining at restaurants serving mussels and clams in silver buckets with tiny silver tongs and cloth napkins.

Meme enrolled me in all kinds of summer enrichment programs, including swimming lessons at the athletic club, ice skating at the mall, classes on beading or clay sculpture, as well as local pageants and parades. I was pampered, spoiled rotten, and I loved it.

I still have the "Best-in-Show" blue ribbon for marching in a community parade dressed like a goldfish. Believe me, it wasn't the sequined leotard, fishnet stockings or chiffon fins that won. Anyone can wear a costume. What pushed me into first place was my mouth taking in and blowing out air like a fish looking back at you from an aquarium when the judges walked by me.

"What are you doing?" asked one of the judges with a clipboard and official "JUDGE" name tag pinned to his pocket.

I maintained my silent, aquatic respiration and added swimming moves that billowed the orange chiffon fins. I also refrained from blinking. Method acting demands sacrifice.

The man stared, shook his head and walked on to look at pirates, hoboes, and clowns. But in the end, my attention to detail and dramatic effect could not be ignored.

"I'm a little worried about that tiny, weird goldfish girl. I'm not sure she can even speak. Let's give her first place."

I loved the life Meme and Daddy Bob shared with me, I loved Meme and Daddy Bob. I could not accept the fact that my dad belonged to them before I did. If they had been as nice to him as they were to me, what in the whole wide world had happened to make him so, so, well, so my dad?

I did not miss my parents, my siblings, the fifteen cent Burger Chef meals, dollar haircuts, and grocery store bought rubber flip-flops during these summer escapes. I got Portland roses not Phoenix cacti, lush landscapes rather than tumbleweeds, and a seemingly bottomless well of love and attention instead of the scarcity of both at home.

By the summer before eighth grade, I had grown to what was to be my full height of 5' 3 1/3". I felt like I was towering over most of the girls and all of the boys in my class. I had become outwardly what I already inwardly felt—statuesque, commanding, someone who's going big places.

I couldn't know then that I would end up short, um petite, and was therefore pre-emptively and wrongly smug about my assured status as a future super model. Afterall, modeling was in my genes. Wanting to be prepared for my destiny, I began studying *Seventeen* magazine. I memorized and idolized every model and mimicked poses in the mirror. Most pre-teen girls read stupid stuff like *Tiger Beat* and became self-conscious and awkward. I became magazine-conscious and a copycat. I strutted rather than traipsed, I stood tall, rather than slumped, and I smiled constantly, as if photographers were around any and every corner. I was in a modeling boot camp for one and worked out diligently and daily.

When my final elementary school summer came and I arrived on my grandparent's doorstep, I put away the childish things like craft classes, swimming lessons, ice skating, and parades and asked Meme to teach me to model and sashay down runways.

Between them, Meme and Daddy Bob had already taught me to knit Barbie doll blankets, make a mean chocolate malt, can peaches, acquire a taste for cottage cheese sprinkled with sugar, order from a menu properly, and in important ways they taught me to enjoy being me. They loved it when I sang, they helped me create backyard musicals, and not only looked at me, but really listened to me, my opinions, my ideas, myself. What I saw reflected back when I looked at them was what I missed at home—being adored, valued, and valuable. That deep reservoir of love irrigated many of my dreams, hopes, and aspirations through past and yet to come emotional drought and doubt.

Meme loved the idea, of course, of teaching me her model ways. She, too, had no reason at this point to believe I would end up being what I choose to call small, but my dad called stunted. If he told me once, he told me a hundred times,

"You're not short, Ronda, they just built the sidewalk too close to your bottom."

Modeling 101 commenced with a visit to the dentist, not—as I had hoped—shopping for fashionable clothes to fit my extra-large self-image.

My parents never took us to the dentist; check-ups must have fallen in the same category as voice lessons, or dance class. A luxury not a necessity. It's like my parents were a cross between put down comedian Don Rickles and Christian Science holy rollers. We had bad teeth and they would make fun of us because of it.

"Your teeth are so bucked you could eat an apple through a picket fence."

They didn't believe in any of those fancy dentist types fixing our teeth. My mother said my crooked teeth gave me character.

Meme said I was enough of a character so she agreed with the dentist that pulling four of my permanent teeth would give the remaining chompers the space to straighten out. I literally gave my eye teeth to become a model.

Next in the curriculum was a trip to the hairdresser to cut my hair in a shorter and more urbane style, a lacquered bubble with bangs and a bow not unlike the lead character in *Hairspray*.

Nonetheless, I felt very Twiggy; though when my dad saw me he stated I more resembled Moe from The Three Stooges. Or maybe it was Ruth Buzzi from *Laugh-In*. He couldn't decide.

While Meme was adjusting my look, Daddy Bob was working on how I spoke. He kept telling me that saying "huh?" instead of "pardon me?" or "yeah" instead of "yes", or "fir" rather than "for" would label me a rube—which I did not understand but, by the way he said it I knew it wasn't good.

One Saturday morning I came to breakfast and found, instead of my cinnamon toast and fresh cut peaches, a row of fifteen quarters.

"Each time you say 'Huh?' when asked a question, I remove a quarter," my grandfather said. "At the end of the day, whatever quarters remain are yours to spend any way you like. "Deal?"

"Deal!"

I couldn't believe the easy money I was going to make that day and was already dreaming about Yardley lip gloss or some other mandatory modeling gear when my grandmother entered the kitchen and mumbled something about breakfast.

"Huh?"

One quarter was quickly removed and put back into my grandfather's pocket.

The sight of that quarter being subtracted, of losing so quickly, scared me straight. I did not lose another, and replaced my grunting, illiterate 'huhs?' with "excuse me" or "pardon me", immediately and consistently. A habit I maintain to this very day.

I now had the teeth, hair, elocution, and lip gloss. I was ready for clothes to model.

I had my eye on a dress I had seen in *Seventeen*. It was light gray with white piping around the bottom of three lace layers that created a flounce skirt. Contrasting vertical white piping and pearl buttons ran along the bodice and the sleeves…and oh! The sleeves! They were sheer with another flounce at the cuff. The young girl modeling it in the magazine was walking a fluffy puppy and being followed by cute clean-cut boys of whom parents, or grandparents, would approve.

I don't know which made me swoon most, the dress or the promise. I looked in the back pages and found the list of stores carrying this dream dress and Meier & Frank was listed. The downtown Portland M&F, the less than twenty minutes away Meier & Frank, the store Meme modeled for—that Meier & Frank!

My model grandmother was more than happy to take me downtown in search of the dress. We found it, she bought it, and I didn't think anything could make me more happy, more fulfilled, or more complete…and then I saw some bright pink patent leather shoes as we were exiting the store through the shoe department. They were Mary Janes with a small heel; perfect as starter model shoes. Showy but not trampy, princess not prostitute, understated but not underestimated. Could be worn to school, could not be worn by anyone else but me.

The showroom light was shining directly on them, or maybe they were refracting that light, magnifying and iridescent-ing the whole shoe department by their brilliance.

I moved toward the shoes until I was close enough to smell them when Meme said, "Gray and pink go well together, they complement each other, don't you think?"

I turned toward her and was unable to form a coherent reply before she said to the salesman, "We'd like to try on these magenta Mary Janes in a size five, please."

I slipped my ped covered feet into the shoes, feeling once more like the little girl who tried on the blue suede slippers. I again imagined myself the princess of the fairy tales I had read. Looking at my feet in beautiful shoes and feeling an electric current of potential from my soles to my soul.

I dared not ask for them, I already had the *Seventeen* magazine dress. I did not need them; they wouldn't match very much of anything else in my dismal clothing collection at home. As the salesman slipped them off my feet and I scrunched up the peds, Meme grabbed my hand and said, "Magenta was your favorite crayon, do you remember?"

My brain was consumed with shoes until Meme mentioned magenta and then, BAM! followed rapidly by YES! I was always pulling magenta out of my Crayola 64 Count box first and using it liberally for everything from trees, to boats, to elephants. Everything in every coloring book from my childhood was awash in pink vividity. Such a happy color fitted with a bright and bold name.

"Color is magic," Meme continued, "it can change your mood, your outlook, boost your energy, or posture. Let's buy these shoes to celebrate the little girl who loved the magenta crayon becoming the model girl you want to be." She hugged me and passed the shoe box to the salesman.

I carried those shoes out of the store and into the world with a deep sense of responsibility and gratitude. The size five magenta patent leather shoes became more than part of a wardrobe to debut my career aspirations. Even now the pink shoes shine in my memory as a reminder of the grace, love, and beauty Meme shared with me.

To be treasured and treated by Meme that day—and so many prior and following days, months, and years—became the standard for how I wanted to be treated and how I would strive to treat others. Although the shoes were beautiful, what prompted my grandmother to buy them for me was more extravagant and extraordinary than their mere outward appearance.

She was the epitome of grace, charm, intelligence, and kindness. From her example I learned that beauty is what beauty does.

I had a model grandmother. Hers were big shoes to fill, but I was determined to make every attempt to do so…no ifs, ands, or 'huhs?'

Put Yourself in My Shoes
Be a Sole Model.
RB

At one point in my checkered and varied career I taught over 400 students a semester the ways and means of becoming a teacher. When I left that position to write, I was unnerved by the loss of impact and immediate gratification of thinking that each day I could make a positive contribution for so many people. For what? To sit alone in a room with a hostile, blank piece of paper? Egad. What had I done?

My husband, after hearing this same wail for the umpteenth time said this, "It doesn't matter if it's 400 students or the one old man I saw you help by picking out the right honeydew melon in the produce section of the grocery store. He lit up like a Christmas tree when you spoke with him. You can make a difference anywhere you are. The number of people isn't the point; the compassion and care you extend is."

What a blessing and privilege to be the one, sole role model for one other person. Each connection will matter and multiply. You don't have to be a celebrity, professional athlete, or successful CEO to be a role model for someone. Simply demonstrating positive behavior and small successes can be enough to inspire others.

It's also important to remember that people are not perfect and neither are role models. Even though as a role model you want to always put your best foot forward, know that you may make mistakes, and that is OK! If you commit to learning from your mistakes, you will grow into the best person and role model you can be.

My grandmother was my sole role model growing up. She has been a part of every class I teach, every speech I make, every book I write, every child I've raised, every friendship I've enjoyed, every achievement, badge, or award I have won. Her influence in my life—if measured by the number of other people I have taught, counseled, or coached—is in the hundreds of thousands.

By striving daily to live your best and most true life, to do good things, to be kind and fair, by embracing every opportunity to tell your unique story so that it might help others, by simply making yourself available to someone seeking advice or acceptance, you, like my grandmother, will be not simply a role model—you will be eternal.

Chapter Five

Sis Boom Saddle Shoes

No helmets, no knee, wrist, or elbow pads,
no mouth guards, no dugouts,
or sidelines. Just a uniform and shoes.

—Cheerleading Tumblr

I was perky, I cared about school spirit, and the bossy pants in me enjoyed yelling at people to "lean to the left, lean to the right, stand up, sit down, fight! fight! fight!"

Four years of high school were not exactly in line with my lofty aspirations. Many of the teachers didn't expect much from the student body and that's pretty much what they got. Classmates brought weed to school, drank beer at lunch, skipped class on unexpected Pacific Northwest sunny days, and were irked by most of the teachers and all of the curriculum. The only part of the whole set-up I did enjoy was the lavish praise I got for simply turning in assignments on time. I morphed into an Eddie Haskell from *Leave It to Beaver* type, all insincere sincerity and smarmy compliments to any and all school authority figures.

"Good morning Miss Disotell, you look great today!"

"Hello Coach, I feel a win coming!"

"Yes, Principal Hash, I agree that some skirts are too short."

It's not that the teachers and staff didn't know I was sucking up, it's just that there were so many students who beleaguered and belittled them that I must have been an irritating relief, like calamine lotion. Crusty, pink, and smelly, but makes the itch bearable. And high school teachers get stung a lot.

I had the same topical effect on my classmates.

I went to one high school "kegger" and a cute boy walked up to me, looked me deep in the eyes as I tried to look back in what I hoped was an alluring way, preparing for a snappy reply like "Yes, I would love to dance with you, or "I think I'll stick with Pepsi," only to have him say,

"You know, you look like you're around thirty."

If this was a pick up line, I braced myself for whatever came out of his mouth next.

He continued that my hair looked too fixed and my sweater was something his mom might wear. He wondered if I might be chaperoning the party.

Another boy that I liked once told me we weren't ever going out because, 'You are the type of girl guys marry, not date'. I was clueless as to what he meant, specifically. Did he think I would look good behind a vacuum cleaner or making chocolate chip cookies?

I was also clueless in general. Assembled with five classmates for a library assignment, I was given the book *Ann Landers Talks to Teens* and told to do a three-minute report on one of the chapters when we got back to the classroom. There were chapters about health, dating, and dealing with parents. I chose the skin care chapter and came upon this sentence:

Contrary to popular opinion, masturbation does not cause acne.

I looked up at my fellow students and asked, "What does masturbation mean?"

Someone spit their gum out, others laughed and choked, and one nice guy took pity and said, not unkindly, "It's when you play with yourself."

"Well, why in the world would playing alone give someone pimples?" I asked, to even more laughter and whoops.

I decided to do my report on the etiquette chapter.

I never went to another high school party. I was apparently un-dateable. I liked playing by myself and I was afraid of drinking beer or doing drugs. My high school years were looking grim and sober.

It's not that people didn't suspect I was drinking or taking drugs. For example, in order to pass geometry, I begged balding, bespectacled, Mr. Fredrickson into letting me do an a2+b2=c2 sketch as Pythagoras. I created a toga from a white sheet and crafted a headband from cardboard stapled with leaves. Pythagoras himself would have been impressed by the sheer drama and force with which I depicted his discovery. My fellow geometry students sat in a silent, slack jawed "she must be high" look when I took my grand, Greek get-up bow. After that no one in class looked at me, ever. They would avert their eyes and stop in mid-sentence, becoming stone cold silent as I walked by to take my seat. It's like they were afraid that whatever weirdness made me dress in a sheet was catching or they thought I was an invading body snatcher. Either way, I was persona non-grata.

Long before YouTube or podcasts, MTV, or Ken Burns, I created a multiple cassette drama series highlighting battles, discoveries, conquests, presidents, and whatever the topic of the week was in Mr. Root's history class. While others read their well-researched and traditional papers, when my turn came, I would bop up to the front of the room, hit play on my tape player, and perhaps a recounting of the Civil War and the injustice of slavery would ensue. As the narrator I did my best southern drawl and added sound effects of doors slamming and feet running as well as "Catch Us If You Can" by The Dave Clark Five as background music. I was taking an alternative route to presenting historical incidents but, as usual, my classmates were unappreciative, dumfounded, non-responsive, possibly scared, and certain I was "tripping."

Finally, after chasing up and down and around what seemed like hundreds of activity avenues, after many diversions and declarations of intentions and inventions designed to find personal greatness, or maybe one friend—boomshakalaka! I tumbled into the ultimate activity that was an amalgam of the passions and promise I had felt were given to me at birth. CHEERLEADING!

Victory was my cry! V-I-C-T-O-R-Y.

W-H-Y?

In my mind, cheer combined creativity, dance, music, acting, leadership, athleticism, popularity, and appreciation… as well as brown and beige saddle shoes. Plus, a preternaturally positive girl like me couldn't help but love being on something called a CHEER squad. I set my sights on spring tryouts at what was my third ninth grade, at the third high school, in the third different neighborhood. And as they say, the third time is the charm.

Over one hundred vivacious, bouncy, smiley, and jumpy girls were scheduled to try out in front of the graduating cheerleaders when I added my name to the roster.

If I made that cut, then I tried out in front of the PE department. If I made that cut, then twelve of us tried out in front of the whole school at an assembly, and then students got to vote on who should have the coveted title of cheerleader. These were big hurdles for a new girl. I didn't know the teachers or the cheerleaders, and I certainly had no one rooting for me. I practiced my routine so often and so hard that my legs from the knee up were bruised from slapping them, "Ready? OK!" Practice may make perfect, but it also hurts. I soldiered on, over and over again, perfecting the snap and timing until I could do the routine in my sleep, and I did, dreaming about winning, dreaming about pom poms, dreaming about my dream.

The hard work and countless hours paid off and I surprisingly made the final cut. I was getting the chance to try out in front of the entire student body. Now, popularity would matter, not skill. And I wasn't even known, let alone popular. On the bright side: so far, it seemed like to know me was to not like me, and since I was new at the school, I wasn't yet unpopular.

My posters for election read **BE-A-MAN, VOTE BEAMAN** and I plastered the school with them. I passed out Beeman's gum to every student I encountered in the halls and I asked to give a mini speech at the end of each of my classes about why I hoped they would vote for me. I was a highly efficient campaigner and continued to practice and politic until the big day finally arrived. At last my big moment had come and I was so nervous that even the inside of my ears were sweating. I was seated on a chair in a line with eleven other girls smack in the middle of the auditorium, bright fluorescent lights were beating down on us, and the marching band was playing the theme from the TV show *Peter Gunn*. I don't remember watching the other candidates, I was in a fog, mentally rehearsing my moves, when my name was finally called, RONDAHHHHH BEEEEMANNNN...it reverberated through the old fuzzy gym speakers and landed in the ears of hundreds of students stuffed onto the bleachers. Heads turned both left and right throughout the seated student body and I could lip read many of them saying, "WHO?" as I ran up to the piece of masking tape that marked where I was supposed to stand and perform.

My smile was wide and genuine as I began my routine. All the practice, all the false starts at singing, or dancing, and even baton twirling were melting away. All my thwarted attempts to be somebody dissipated. The gym fell away. Hundreds of students and teachers fell away. There was just me and *Two Bits! Four Bits!* I felt and thought, for sure, 'This is it! This is what I have been waiting for, hoping for, praying for... this is my thing.'

And then.

The final cross-T-land-on-one-knee jump...it was a risky move, an innovation I added that would either make me a cheer champ or chump. Up, up I rose, buoyed by enthusiasm and hamstrings, out went both legs in opposite directions as I reached with outstretched arms toward both toes and then flew rapidly down to the soft and graceful landing which I had practiced hundreds of times.

But on this day when I did land, I was lost in the revelry of what I felt was my moment and failed to ease up as I came back down. A practically supersonic **THUD** hit those unforgiving floors and every student, teacher, and custodian in the audience gasped in unison. They were sure I had shattered my kneecap. Heck, I thought for a moment I had shattered my kneecap! The other cheer candidates covered their mouths in sympathetic pain and mortification. Maybe even a little joy, as for sure I would not win now. I stayed arms out, one knee down, smiling for what seemed a very long time, and then I couldn't help it, I began to laugh. I stood up, brushed my beginning-to-bruise knee off, saw no blood, no smashed kneecap, so I did a little curtsy to the silent and then instantaneously cheering and applauding audience. I waved to the crowd and ran back to my chair in line with the other cheery hopefuls.

Well much to everyone's, including my, amazement I won a spot on the squad! Surely not because of my prowess, my posters, or my public speaking. I believe it was the THUD that won it for me. I got the sympathy vote.

Donning my cheer sweater embroidered with my name on the sleeve, the culotte skirt in royal blue, and the bright yellow crew socks that highlighted my beige and brown saddle shoes was not about high jumps or splits. Cheerleading for me was about being someone other people counted on to inspire them, to get them excited, to help them win. I relished every routine, every assembly, all the summer cheer camps, and the positive public persona we were expected to project. I loved it all. Except the splits. I never liked or could do the splits.

Each time I entered the drab, gray bricked, windowless building that was Hazen High School, I knew what my mission was and why I was born; to be cheerful, to greet all equally, to be perky and encouraging, to be a jumping, yelling, rhyming, clapping, pom-pomming role model of enthusiasm, spirit, and PEP!

My saddle shoes survived Seattle rain and mud during football games and scuffed dozens of unforgiving hardwood floors in gyms across the state. I sang hundreds of national anthems wearing them, and yelled "Ready? OK!" hundreds more. I wore those scruffy, waterlogged shoes in my early steps toward becoming a leader with a Go Team! Go! attitude whether I was winning, losing, or landing with a thud.

Put Yourself in My Shoes
2 - 4 - 6 - 8
who do you appreciate?
RB

I know I painted a pretty positive and popular picture about my time as a cheerleader, but it wasn't all cute uniforms and handsone.

By putting yourself out there—in any way, be it excelling at work, club pickle ball champ, or fastest selling cookies at the bake sale—you're gonna rile those who didn't win, those who never entered, and sometimes those who don't like you because everyone else likes you.

When I won the election for cheerleader, suddenly people I didn't even know were complaining that I never moved my head because I was afraid to mess up my hair, or saying my hands were too small to see from up in the stands, or my voice was too high. They claimed I was so fake smiling, and on, and on. It hurt. Not gonna lie.

It's hard not to get discouraged. But look at that word… it means giving away your bravery, you are dissing courage, your courage, and that means that you have let those who are not brave enough to fulfill their own goals beat you.

Worst phrase in the English language? "Must be nice."

Must be nice to have that job.

Must be nice to buy expensive shoes.

Must be nice to live where you live, be who you are, have what you have.

The person declaring 'it must be nice' is diminishing all the blood, sweat, and tears, the sleepless night, the years of school, the risks, obstacles, and challenges it took to get where you are and who you are. Never abandon a passion or a purpose because of outside criticism or lack of a cheerleader. Be your own cheerleader. Believe in your team of talents. Your soul is rooting for you—Sis Boom Bah!

High School Shoe Glossary

Nordstrom	Where the popular—read wealthy—girls bought shoes and where I claimed mine were from. Just not the Nordstrom in our town.
JCPenney	Where my shoes were actually from.
Sears	See above.
Red vintage pumps	Goodwill find, platform shoes from 1950's era, tried for a little while to be bohemian.
Brown suede ballerinas	Flats worn with knee high argyles when I tried being the iconoclast.
Moccasin	Cause of mocking; worn once.
Surfer shoes	Thick-soled, navy blue canvas shoes, unattractive, but better looking than my surfer bangs.
Silver T-straps	Prom shoes. Low heeled (short date).
Rubber duckies	Yellow rain boots used consistently for cheerleading in the rain. One demerit if you forgot them.
Loafers	Slip on leather shoe that usually featured a penny. Or what my dad called me because I didn't have a part-time job.

Mules	Backless shoes that slipped forward ahead of my foot and made me look like an ass.
Sling back	Again with the foot falling out. This time the back-strap drops, and I twist my ankle at dance.
Lace ups	Sturdy—could jazz them up with colored shoelaces—and at least they stayed on when walking.
Heels	Made my calves look leaner, my leg longer, attractive to boys pretending to be men like I was pretending to be a woman by wearing them. Also, a synonym for many of those same boys who think they are real men.
Wedge	Safer than wearing sling backs, a compromise design for those who twist ankles.
Army boots	Perfect with the popular navy surplus bell bottoms. Comfortable, sturdy, cheap, everything a guy wants in a shoe. Maybe they are on to something.
Princess pumps	Bought after being nominated for homecoming queen. I lost. Should have found Queen Pumps.
Go-go boots	White short boots like Goldie Hawn wore on the TV hit *Laugh-In*. On me they were comical.

Chapter Six

These Boots Were Made For Talking

Shoes are the first adult machines we are given to master.

—Nicholson Baker

My plan was to major in Mary Tyler Moore.

During my senior year of high school my parents took the family on a Sunday drive. It turned out to be a ninety-mile one-way life changer. The destination was a state university. "Let's take a walk around campus," my dad said in an eerily cheery manner. We walked around actual ivy-covered buildings and past big rise dormitories for a whole ten minutes before my dad turned to me and asked, "What do you think?"

"I don't know," I said, and my dad replied, "You'll like it," and dropped the letter of application he had filled out as my surrogate in the campus mailbox. He walked away as I stared at the mailbox, wondering what had just happened.

He had for many years filled out all our medical clearances for sports or scouts, signing them with various doctors' names he found in the phone book. He had posed as an uncle when teachers called to speak with our father about any number of problems; and told a census taker that his job was as a bodyguard for Frank Sinatra. Writing an essay for college entrance as a seventeen-year-old girl was par for the course.

The essay must have been a doozy and God only knows what he said I said because less than a year later I was surrounded by boxes and hearing Carol King songs booming from almost every other room in my dorm hall. The other girls in this dorm looked like what my dad called "dirty hippies", but I was wearing a navy blue and white A-line dress with white tights and bright red, gold buckled flats. I chose the shoes for my first day as a co-ed because they were as close to ruby slippers as I could get. I was anticipating being nervous but secretly celebrating the promise 'There's no place like home.' Click-click-click.

Despite whatever lofty goals my paternal essay may have stated, I myself had come to college to be an actress, a drama major to be exact. Or Mary Tyler Moore, to be more exact. My parents, on the other hand, told me they were sending me to college to meet a better quality of potential husband than my original post-secondary plan, a community college degree that insured my place as a stewardess. My dad quickly and thoroughly kiboshed what I believed to be a glamorous and high-minded career choice in one fell swoop.

"So, you want to be a waitress?"

"No."

"Want to clean up after people when they get sick and throw up?"

"No."

"Then you don't want to be a stewardess. It's just a flying waitress job. Besides, you're too short."

I wore the same moving to college red shoes to my first day of my new-life-as-a-drama-major and breezed into the

Introduction to Acting class as if I was wearing a chiffon gown and silver slippers. And tiara.

Upon entering I was not greeted by my expectations of beautiful starlets, handsome leading men, or even intriguing character actor types. Not a Karl Malden or James Garner in sight. Where, I wondered, were the young Cary Grants or the next Audrey Hepburns?

What I did see was un-showered and unshaved faces and legs, disheveled students of all shapes and sizes, mostly out of shapes and big sizes, lying on the floor, sitting cross legged, or with their backs against the small stage that was dimly lit in the front of the dingy room. My dad's words rang in my ears, "dirty hippies." I resisted the urge to run, in my red shoes, right out the door.

It's not like my fellow thespians were all that enamored with me either.

Dressed in a red vest, red gaucho pants, neon yellow blouse and tights, and those red shoes, with my flipped hair and full makeup, I was totally channeling my Plan B to be Marlo Thomas. The few eyes that did glance at me laughed mildly, shrugged their shoulders, poked another student, and pointed at me or did a double take. One guy said, just loud enough for me to hear, "Whoa! It's Ronald McDonald!"

I took a chair from the middle of the muddle of students and carried it to the back of the room. I piled my notebook, acting text, and purse on the small kidney shaped piece of wood that served as a desk and slid in.

Fifteen minutes went by with no teacher. I pretended to write some notes, keeping my head down but listening to the acting chatter around me, topics like auditions for plays coming up, theatre troupes forming, how alcohol can loosen up inner character work. 'The last thing these guys needed is liquid courage,' I thought. They were already showing plenty of bravery and abandon just by their clothing choices.

"Ring! Ring! Riiiiiiiing!" From the right side of the stage entered a rumpled, long haired, unkempt portly man of about forty. His clothes and face were baggy, and he plodded to the center of the stage still yelling "RING!"

"I am an alarm clock." Everyone up and at 'em."

At this prompt every acting student in the room, with one red and yellow clad exception, started to yawn, stretch, moan, and pull themselves out of imaginary beds. It was faintly reminiscent of a scene I'd seen in *Night of the Living Dead,* but these zombies were my classmates and I was afraid, very afraid. I was in fact paralyzed by fear, watching in horror as their bodies contorted and crouched and crawled out of imaginary beds.

Suddenly the professor yelled, "We are off to the zoo, I want to see some animals."

Instantly the room was filled with a cacophony of elephant bugles, seal flapping, lions and tiger and bears, 'oh why?'

The reckless and blatant disregard for self-image which the other students were displaying put me in full fright and flight mode. I put my head on my desk and started pushing my pretty red shoes, covering my cold feet, against the floor, moving the desk ever so slowly and silently toward the exit door, stage left.

"Hey, you!" the professorial wannabe Alfred Hitchcock yelled. "YOU! MISS PRISS."

There was no doubt in my mind whom he was addressing. I slowly raised my head from the desk to look up and at him.

"What are you supposed to be?"

In what I still think was a stroke of acting genius showing creative character development I replied, "I am a baby monkey, this is my first day in a cage and I am feeling scared and shy."

I admit, becoming a wimpy chimp was more confessional than creative but the dramatic diversion worked.

The professor stared blankly at me for a moment, shook his head, and then went back to yelling at everyone else to now imagine getting on a bus for the West Indies. I scooted rapidly toward the back of the room, gathered my things, and ran as fast as my little red shoes could carry me to the registrar's office to change my major.

I chose Communications. As rattled as I was by realizing the acting life was not for me, by facing the fact that I lacked the self-esteem and probably talent of an actress, I jumped into what I thought would be the next best thing. Being a communications major would allow for some performance opportunities without the drama. No ad-libbing or imaginary zoo animals. But, there were still cameras, microphones, radio, and television scripts. All good.

I became a student television director. I produced public service programs, announced on a campus radio station, did the nightly televised campus news, and by senior year was considered a top recruit for a local, if not national broadcast job. In order to be hired at a network I would first have to get an internship to prove I could do work beyond a college classroom.

My advisor found an opportunity at a local radio station and lined me up for an interview.

I shopped for a Jessica Savitch type suit. She was the anchor at NBC, she had started in radio, and she was being taken seriously even though female and blonde. I hoped to follow in her footsteps. I chose a chocolate brown dress printed with small red roses and paired the dress with brown suede boots that made me feel like I had hit, or for sure would hit, the big time. They were rust brown with a gold zipper on the inside leg of each boot, running from my ankle to the top of the boots, just below my knee. Big. Girl. Boots.

Excited for my interview and sitting in the reception area of the station, I was holding onto a cassette player and mini-speakers ready to play my sample advertisements and highlight some local reporting. My resume was folded into a 45-record sleeve with all my accomplishments highlighted as "Ronda's Record" in keeping with my objective to be a station intern. I had practiced anticipated questions, and droll but intelligent answers, and was silently rehearsing some more when I heard the receptionist say, "The general manager will see you now."

Before I explain what happened next, I need to complete the description of how I looked. Besides my new dress and boots, I had an expression on my face not unlike Disney's Bambi. Dreamy, hopeful, untainted, and naïve...a baby deer in headlights. I was all those things, to be sure. I was a girl scouting, junior princess, cheerleading, mannerly, pleasant young girl with big dreams and killer boots prepared to slay the interview and eager to get on my adult way.

What I wasn't prepared for was the general manager's welcoming remark as I strode in to shake hands, "Well, if I had known you looked like this, I would have brought you in here sooner."

'If I had known you were a jerk, I wouldn't have spent so much money on my boots.' I thought to myself as my stomach sorta went sour.

I handed him my resume, smiled and laughed politely, as other girls had told me they did when something they wanted was being dangled in front of them by an older, in charge man. Maybe dangled isn't the best word? Or maybe it is.

I sat down and began to set up my cassette of advertising samples and he said, "A little romantic music, I hope?"

I persisted, pretending I didn't hear him, and replied, "I thought you would like to listen to some of the copy I have written for national and local accounts."

"I don't think that's necessary. Great photo on your resume, you look capable of everything I need you to do around here."

I sat looking at him, unsure, to be sure, of how to respond.

"Let's get you started right away. You can do the Croatian Hour on Sunday nights from 6:00 – 9:00 p.m. Then you and I will do sales calls together during the week and write the copy for the ads we sell. Have the girl out front give you the paperwork. See you here, Sunday night, at 5:45 p.m." With that he stood up, motioned me through his office door, and turned right as I went straight ahead to the reception desk. I was out of sight but not earshot when I heard one of the guys down the hall ask him if he hired me.

"I didn't hire her; I hired her legs."

I knew I was not a great beauty—my dad had told me so. I knew my legs were regular legs, attached to skinny, bony feet. I wasn't supposed to hear the general manager's retort and it stopped me in my tracks. I felt a queasy rush of embarrassment and flush of heat that rose to my face. In that small radio station hallway, for the first time, I realized there was a kind of power in the world—and that I didn't have it. Or the power I did have was not tied, as I had thought, to the organ between my ears.

I decided I would take the job, use it to move up and out, and in the meantime, I would wear pants to work.

I wore the same boots, this time with loose jeans tucked into them, to my first Sunday night Croatian Hour. I sat in a booth with a Slavic gentleman who announced his music, did his ads, and tossed me a copy of the English version to be read following his remarks. I was a radio personality and translator for those not speaking Croatian in my college town, meaning possibly everyone but Milos and his family.

Milos:

"Dojdi na svirkački buden pazar!"

Me:

"Come to Piggly Wiggly Market!"

Despite the weirdly guilty feeling that came with accepting a job from a guy who did not care about the leg work I had done to be qualified, I was employed in broadcasting, I was wearing headphones and speaking into a commercial, not a college microphone, and I was broadcasting off campus and into the world, or at least the Slavic speaking world.

I was the first communication major at my school to get this internship. What the boss thought of my legs may have been the reason I got the job, but I was determined it was my talent and worth that would keep me there. I was going to use this experience to get a suede-booted leg up and be a step ahead. Not to mention, getting to a place in life where I could kick guys like the general manager to the curb!

Put Yourself in My Shoes
Everything you want is one step outside your comfort zone.
RB

I wore pigtails and pink and gray oxfords to the open auditions for all the college plays being produced my freshman year in college. I read a piece from Neil Simon's Star Spangled Girl like it was written for and about me. I share this not because I felt that confident at the time, (who knew it's possible to sweat behind your knees?) but because despite the wet and weak knees, I actually made the call backs for all the shows. In other words, all the directors wanted me to read again for their plays—six of them.

I still remember finding my name on all the rosters and thinking immediately, "I am just too busy to do this. I don't have the time."

And I never went back. For the auditions or to idea of being an actor. The story that I made all the callbacks but was just too busy to follow through was easier to boast, share, and explain than if I had gone back, tried, and, in the end, didn't get a part.

It's called flight or fight, and I flew. And I have been in the same situation over and over again, whether an internship, a job, or a relationship. I have fled from someone's rude remark, a difficult role, or a tough situation more times than I like to admit. It's not that you know at the time that you're copping out, but once you back away from a hurdle, a dream, a risk, a fear, or practically anything, and you choose comfort and safety, once you cop out, you never, ever forget it and it sort of makes you not like yourself as much. Which is a way tougher thing to carry around than trying but not winning a part, a job, or a love. You know when you cop out. You know when fear won. And you know you became less than you could be. It's not easy but you have to tell yourself, "World, I got this." Whatever "this" is. Because you do; you can.

It's time for you to step out of those old, worn, comfortably broken shoes and begin stretching a new pair, relaxing and shifting the leather as it heats to your body's temperature and your foot molds it into a new shape that will take you where you really want to go.

Chapter Seven

Monkey See-Monkey Shoe

It's really fun to put yourself into a character–
into shoes you wouldn't normally be in.

—Billie Eilish

It was essential to wear big hairy shoes with room for semi-opposable, tree-gripping, long toes.

I left the jungle of a media career in LA for graduate school in the west Texas plains and created a singing gorilla telegram company I named Shenanigrams. There were dozens of companies doing singing, kissing, even stripping telegrams on the west coast, but the craze had not arrived in the Lone Star state. Lots of wind, churches, sweet tea and mesquite BBQ, but no one in Lubbock or at Texas Tech had ever received a singing telegram until I donned my gorilla suit and shoes. Shenanigrams hit like a west Texas tornado and made me so much money, I was singing for more than my supper, rent, tuition, and car.

Within a few months, I built Shenanigrams from a single singing gorilla to a company of over twelve that included magicians, superheroes, and clowns. I recruited talent from the university, where there were many willing performers, juvenile crazies, and students in need of money who had already cashed out their plasma allotment.

I spared no expense on my gorilla gear, it came direct from a Hollywood costume supplier. The body was bulky, the fur was long and shaggy, as was the face, with two little eye holes for me to see and an open mouth so I could breathe. I added a big red and white polka dot bow and a red tutu over the fur. The dainty dance and demure demeanor inspired by the feminine accoutrements was pure slap stick and I, or rather the gorilla, became a local celebrity.

I bounded into each job singing a standard intro song to the tune of "If They Could See Me Now":

"You wanted spice in life, so baby here I am
Your very own gorilla singing telegram
From friends who said no other present would do,
They sent me here to make a monkey of you."

For each telegram I wrote a special poem based on the recipient's hobbies, age, or other information gleaned from the giver of the "gift." Doing the song, reading the poem, grabbing my fifty-dollar check, and running out to my car took less than three minutes. I was the hardest working gorilla in show business and maybe the highest paid, earning more in minutes than the era's average minimum wage for ten hours.

I did gigs all over the city. I, or rather my ape alter ego, sat on the police chief's lap, ran fingers through the mayor's hair, unloosed the tie of the university football coach, broke the stride of the local news anchor on air, and was nominated homecoming queen by one of the university's fraternities.

There were low notes, to be sure. One night I got a call from a man who wanted to hire my popular clown character, Buckets. Buckets carried a big bucket, was dressed in full clown gear, white face, red nose, and flapping shoes. Buckets would enter the party belting out the tune "I'm bringing in the rain, just bringing in the rain" leading everyone in the room to believe they were gonna get hit with water. Then, as the song ended Buckets would throw the contents of the pail at our recipient. Everyone would duck, then scream, then laugh as confetti flew. Everyone loved Buckets.

As the call to book the clown 'gram progressed, I asked the gentleman on the phone what the occasion was.

"No occasion."

"So, just a party for fun?" I asked, taking notes for the poem I would write.

"No party."

Pause.

"OK, well how many people will be there?"

"Just me."

Buckets the clown was about to be hired by Creepy the caller.

"You want the clown character to come to your house for no party, no guests, for what reason?"

"I like clowns."

Click.

But most disturbing, and to this day the only unpaid singing telegram I did, was for a 90-year-old woman at a nursing home. Her daughter called long distance and asked if I would accept a mailed in payment, she did not have a credit card, and sing Happy Birthday to her mother. I could not turn down singing for a lonely 90-year-old with no family nearby.

I pulled on my gorilla suit and shoes, jumped in my car, found the home, parked the car, swung out, smoothed out my tutu, adjusted my bow, and started to wave at the seniors sitting in rocking chairs on the front porch. From the looks of it, only the wind was moving their chairs to and fro. The slightly moving seats were occupied by gray, somnambulant, elderly, men and women—corralled, dumped maybe, at a holding tank 'til they died—and here was me, or should I say a gorilla in a tutu, frenetically waving at them as I pranced by in my hairy shoes. Not one smile, or wave, or even nod from anyone. I wanted to turn and lope myself back to the car and out of there but, duty called. A faraway daughter was counting on me to brighten her mother's birthday, so I continued past the rocking chair riders and into reception.

The haggard and bored look on the RN's face when I entered signaled, 'Oh another dressed up gorilla' but her voice said, "May I help you?"

My face, under the mask, screamed, 'YES, please tell me to leave' but my voice sang, "I am here to see Mildred!" with arms open wide and hips swaying left and right.

"Follow me."

I wished she had said "walk this way" because it could have been high hilarity to imitate her lumbering. Instead, I did a slow skip behind her, waving at the people in the rooms we passed, who never saw me because they were staring straight ahead and into their past, or paralyzed by *The Merv Griffin Show* or *Match Game.*

We finally arrived at Mildred's room. She was laying under a lavender colored blanket and her meal tray was pulled over her lap, showcasing a stale and crumpled cupcake with a previously burned candle leaning off to the side.

"Mildreeeed" I sang, a little too loud, my sadness at the scene taking the form of over-enthusiasm and volume.

Mildred did not look up, did not look over, did not move.

I came to the side of her bed and, as best as my beady gorilla slit eyes could muster, looked right at her and said softly, "Your daughter wants you to know she is wishing you a happy birthday."

Mildred's eyes shifted a bit groggily and looked at my shaggy, fur covered face, then her eyes slowly turned back to the game show blasting television.

I patted her hand and laid the Shenanigrams poem card on her bed.

I couldn't do more than stumble out of Mildred's room, I felt like a helium balloon, the festiveness and billow diminishing with each moment. I passed each room and caught undisguised glimpses of being old. Once my furry feet were again outside the nursing home I ran back to my car, pulled off my mask, and cried all the way home.

The majority of recipients of the singing telegrams lit up, laughed, danced with me, or remained in a state of shock during the performance, but it's Mildred I remember most vividly. She is my reminder that every show comes to an end, every performance has a finale, every life has a story, and I was trying to make mine a page-turner.

Shenanigrams had so much monkey business that characters were added almost weekly.

I did Dolly Parton wearing cowboy boots and denim, as well as a Dallas Cowboy Cheerleader in white go-go boots. Both get ups included big blonde wigs and lots of makeup. My choice of outrageous, overdone dress up sometimes backfired because in Lubbock I ran into offices or banks or parties to do a performance and there were already lots of women there who actually looked like Dolly or a cowboy cheerleader—for real. This was west Texas where hair was big; and so were the diamonds, boots, and fringe bloused breasts.

Still my red skirted, big footed gorilla was the major money maker and reigning queen of the jingle.

The jobs continued to pour in, and I added balloon bundles, roses, candy, specialty items requested by the client and marked all that up even more. On Valentine's Day alone I delivered one telegram and box of candy or single red rose every twenty minutes from 5:30 a.m. until 10:00 p.m. I made thousands of dollars just that day when it was all said and sung.

Singing telegrams in a mask or makeup gave me wide berth to go bananas and release the Broadway baby I had been bottling up inside for most of my life. I was juiced by making people laugh, helping celebrate special occasions, being the focal point and highlight at the events, and was consistently jazzed knowing that my energy and enthusiasm was contagious and celebrated.

I left big footprints in Texas, or at least when I was wearing the singing telegram costume I did. And yet, it was always me behind that mask, me with the courage and hope, me singing the song, me—who had what her dad called the ugliest feet—who was the one wearing the hairy, even uglier gorilla feet to become an entertainer, finance a graduate degree, and me who was finally ready to swing free from my tangled family tree.

Put Yourself in My Shoes
For me, with a character, you start with the shoes.
—Oscar Issac
RB

What costume do you wear? What character's shoes are you trying to fill? What mask do you put on daily, monthly, yearly?

If we are insecure, we might hide behind the mask of name-dropping. If we are unsure of our power, we can hide behind the mask of being a bully. If we don't think the world loves us, we can hide behind a mask of hostility. We mask the debt we've incurred to pay for lifestyles we can't afford; we pretend things are fine at work when our jobs are on the line; we pretend things are OK in our marriages when there is distance. We put on fake smiles, laugh when we want to cry, and spend too much time attempting to impress people we don't care about by being a person we don't even like or know.

There are a few reasons we should shed our masks. The first is to live to our potential. We have to bring all of who we are to what we do. There are numerous people who have our same skillsets, or maybe an even better one. But none of these people bring the same background, history, and spirit to the job that you do. That's something they can't match. The irony is that we often mask that unique part of ourselves at work and lose our greatest potential.

It is also exhausting to live an inauthentic life. You put on a mask. Or two. Or ten. Then take a few off. Then put a couple more on. Oscar Wilde said it best, "Be yourself, everyone else is taken."

We weren't born with masks. We put them on, so we can take them off. Start with this simple exercise: Think about a negative message you have held onto. Ask yourself: "Is it true?" More than likely, the answer is no. And if it is not, then you have to ask these questions: "Why am I carrying that message? If I put it down, what would happen?"

As the poet E.E. Cummings wrote, "The greatest battle we face as human beings is the battle to protect our true selves from the self the world wants us to become."

Think about the masks you wear and commit to taking them off. Take it from me, the former dancing gorilla, you will breathe much easier!

Chapter Eight

High Roller in Flats

The flat shoe makes the woman equal of men.

—Karl Lagerfeld

I was paid $100,000 to be with Alex Trebek for two days.

I was living a drive away from Burbank, had some free time, an empty bank account and a head filled with higher education minutia. In other words, I thought I was a perfect contestant for the daytime game show, *High Rollers*, hosted by Alex Trebek. I decided to audition.

I drove to an office complex on the Sunset Strip and was led to an overstuffed and stuffy office and told to wait. The photos on the wall were like a game show Who's Who. Wink Martindale, Gene Rayburn, Monty Hall and Bob Barker, among them. There was certainly a "type." Plastered and cropped hair, capped teeth, wide smile, and always a pinky ring.

Stacks of papers dotted every surface, cigarette butts with red lipstick stains on the filters were in the ashtray, and venetian blinds that had never been dusted hung over yellowed glass windowpanes. The office was musty and the chair I was asked to sit in was stained with, what? Flop sweat from nervous, hopeful contestants? Dripping Aqua Velva hair gel from the hosts? The office was straight out of a B movie detective office. This office was where the behind-the-scenes toil and trials were done to populate the glamorous work of the Ken doll hosts. No contestants? No show.

After a few minutes of waiting and wondering how, and more to the point, why I get myself into situations like this, an older woman dressed in an orange flowered muumuu, lavished with a bright red schmear of lipstick, and sporting a lit cigarette hanging from her mouth, breezed in saying, "Sorry, we are casting for multiple shows today, who are you again? What show are you trying out for?" she asked as she picked up a big stack of loosely piled papers.

Never one to miss an opportunity, I replied in what I attempted and thought to be a bright, personality plus delivery, "I could be on any of your shows." I think I winked and gave her a pointed finger pistol shot.

This stopped her paper shuffling, and she gave me the once over and harrumphed, not gently, "What show did they tell you this interview was for?" She glared at me as if I had just added another stain on the chair. I wondered to myself what the job requirements must be for her gig. Good eye rolls, disdain for us suckers who want to win money, a world worn soul?

"*High Rollers*."

At the time, *High Rollers* was the number one game show on daytime television. Two contestants competed. The object was to remove the digits, one through nine from a game board by rolling an oversized pair of dice. The answers were usually multiple choice, true/false, or yes/no. The first contestant to buzz in received the chance to answer; and answering correctly won control. If that contestant did not answer correctly, control went to the opponent.

Once in control, a contestant could either roll the dice himself/herself or pass them to the opponent. After rolling, the contestant had to remove one or more digits from the board that added up to the total on the dice. For example, if a 10 was rolled, the contestant could remove any available combination that added up to that number: 1-9, 2–8, 3–7, 4–6, 1–2–7, 1–3–6, 1–4–5, 2–3–5, or 1–2–3–4, providing that none of the digits within the combination had already been removed. Contestants banked prizes by removing individual numbers or combinations of them, depending on the rules. I had seen players on the show win prizes that ranged from typical game show gifts (furniture, appliances, trips, etc.) to more unusual items such as a collection of musical dolls or fifty-two Sunday Kentucky Fried Chicken dinners. To win, you needed to know a lot about current events, be somewhat knowledgeable about trivia, and be fast enough to beat your opponent to slapping the buzzer.

Ascertaining I was a *High Rollers* hopeful, the smoking muumuu lady pulled a piece of paper from one of her piles, never looking up at me, and said,

"What team does Steve Garvey play for?"

"Dodgers."

"How many musicians are in the Beach Boys?"

"Depends on if you think Mike Love is a musician." I laughed.

World weary woman looked at me over the paper, sighed, and kept going.

"What was Thomas Edison's middle name?"

"Alvin."

The questions were my first clue that you didn't need to be a mental giant to compete on one of the game shows. As if reading my mind, the muumuu woman said, "You can have a modicum of intelligence and still do well on *High Rollers*."

What, exactly, was she saying to me? I thought for sure the answer was Alvin.

"What we really want is teeth," she continued.

"Teeth?"

"Big, wide smiles, showing lots of teeth. No one in TV Land wants to see a loser, no one wants to see a poor sport... even when you lose you must be happy to be a loser."

'That explains some of the host photos on your wall', I thought.

"Makes sense!" I chirped, smiling from ear to ear and feeling like those hapless beauty pageant participants who must go to the same hair stylists as game show hosts and who answer, "I hope for world peace and a hot tub in everyone's backyard," no matter what the question.

"We'll call you." And with that she waved her hand over her head and toward the door.

I had driven through LA traffic for over four hours for this five-minute interview and was leaving without knowing whether I was smiley enough or not. 'I should have told her I was a cheerleader in high school,' I thought. I should have explained my experience behind and in front of a camera, I should have just put my head back, hooked my fingers on both sides of my mouth and pulled open for a full teeth frontal view instead of answering any questions.

Almost six weeks later I got the call to be at Studio 2 in Burbank at NBC the next day. The. Next. Day. I was to bring at least four changes of clothing, be prepared to spend the night and was not guaranteed I would get on during this round of shows.

I picked through my clothing for something that made me look intelligent and competitive, and something that would highlight my teeth. I chose a couple of bright red dresses, a kelly green silk blouse, and, most importantly, beige patent leather mid-heel pumps that resembled what Vanna White wore on *Wheel of Fortune*. They matched everything and didn't interrupt the line of your leg. Or so my mother told me. In other words, your legs looked even longer, there was no visible shoe line.

Viewers think the contestants go home, sleep, change clothes, have a good breakfast, and begin each day with a fresh start. Nope. Usually five shows a day are filmed and I was told if I get on air early in the morning and kept winning, I would be there eight or nine hours. As a contestant I would have only have fifteen minutes to change clothes before filming the next episode.

And, so it was. My name was drawn from a dozen other hopeful contestants in the first round so I was to face the reigning *High Rollers* champ in only the second match of the morning.

Alex was backstage waiting for the theme song and his introduction, I sat on my stool behind the buzzer, and the current champ looked over and whispered, "Good luck."

"Thank you."

"You'll need it." He smiled a menacing smile and then held it for what seemed like five minutes, staring right at me. One of his eyes was a bit bigger and seemed to focus on a spot a bit above my head. He looked a little like Marty Feldman in *Young Frankenstein*.

At long last I was able to break eye contact with one of my opponent's eyes when I saw Alex Trebek enter to my right, attaching his microphone as he glided up to the green felted *High Rollers* table. His suit and tie were impeccable, his demeanor warm and inviting, as if this was his first-time show, and we were his first participants.

"You're on!" the stage manager yelled, pointed at Alex, and off we went. Before I knew what was happening, I missed the first question. I was so disarmed by Alex, fascinated by the set, and unsteeled by my opponent Igor that I didn't even hear the first question. I hit the buzzer late and it made a Gawd awful sound. I couldn't stop myself; I imitated the buzz sound in all its bass crankiness and made a face to match, scrunched, shoulders up tongue out. Mr. Trebek was taken aback and I blurted out "It's not bad enough you lose, then you get insulted by the buzzer?" Alex laughed and asked me to make the sound again. This time the audience laughed. I was on a roll. I won the match. And the next match and the next match. I had the rhythm of the buzz-in first and fast down pat, I could anticipate what Alex was going to say by intently watching his mouth and guessing the next word before it was uttered. This gave me a distinct advantage over other contestants who would wait for the entire question to be asked.

I won the next six matches and was stacking up winnings including a trip to the New Jersey boardwalk, a fur coat, signed Picasso and Dali paintings, washers and dryers, one of the first Apple computers, jewelry, and antiques. All the liberal arts and general studies from college were paying off as I continued to answer random questions on everything from politics, to history, to current events, and astronomy. I felt like Alex's co-host, I had been on so long. Other contestants were dreading being called for their turn, as they were afraid to face my lightening quick reflexes and seemingly unending store of inane knowledge. I was definitely running the table and the big, fluffy dice were being good to me.

We wrapped (I was also picking up show biz lingo) for the day and I was to be back the next morning with my change of clothes and fresh face.

I drove hours home in my newly won fur coat and my old tennis shoes. I had been wearing heels all day and my feet were killing me.

The next day I arrived at the studio, hung up my new round of clothes and donned red suede flats with black trim for the benefit of my tired tootsies. They were flat, they were soft, but they were red and fierce. I walked out ready to win. The *High Rollers* rule was a person could only be on the show for eight wins, and I was on six, so I knew my run was almost over and I, for sure, wanted to leave undefeated.

Alone on the stage with Alex, who was a gentleman and a calming presence, I prepared to meet my next opponent as the music swelled and the red light flashed above the cameras.

"From Annapolis, Maryland, meet Vietnam War veteran, purple heart recipient, and father of six, Commander so and so."

I wasn't listening to the exact wording because I could see the Commander, in full regalia, in the wings, ready for combat.

The Commander strode out and up to me—shaking my hand from his 6'5" officer self, looking down at my 5'3 1/3" champion self—and said, "You've had a good run."

'This must be how David felt when he faced Goliath,' I thought.

The audience in studio and at home can see our mouths moving on camera, but the music is up, our microphones are down, and it looks like we are being pleasant.

Lacking a slingshot, I rose up on my red flats and gave it back to him, "You're right, and it's not over yet."

I shrank a little when the questions seemed absurdly and pointedly to be about geography, oceans, Strait of Hormuz, and the like. They might as well have been asking him about his home address in Annapolis, his Zodiac sign, or his children's middle names.

No clue.

The buzzer and right answer went time and time again to him, and he would roll and get valuable prizes added to his winning column. When finally, there were only two numbers, a five and a two left on the board, he passed the dice to me, smiled condescendingly, saluted and said, "Goodbye."

If I rolled a seven—any combination of seven—it was winner take all, if I rolled anything else that didn't equal seven, it was "Dismissed, Seaman Beaman."

I took the dice from the towering Commander and nervously jiggled those enormous dice, blew on them, oblivious to the cheering, chanting audience, and yelled the only dice rolling motto I knew, "Baby needs new shoes" as I trundled the oversize, plush dice of destiny.

I watched the dotted cubes tumble in slow motion, bounce off the wood trim, come just as slowly rolling back my way, teetering, waffling, and at last stopping together in the middle of the green felted *High Rollers* table on a…four and a three…I WON! As much as I couldn't believe it, the Commander had lost the battle. He couldn't believe it either and was as gobsmacked as I imagine Goliath was when he got the slingshot cargo right in his smacker. The tall Commander had a short stay on *High Rollers*.

This time it was me saluting him on his way out, stage left.

I was the eighth biggest winner in *High Rollers'* history. Moving vans arrived at my door for the next six months delivering what I had won, including a trestle table from the 1700's that is now in the library of my alma mater. People would recognize me at the market, or restaurant and come up saying, "I saw you on *High Rollers.*" For fifteen minutes I was more than famous in my own mind.

My life was turning out to be very much like a *High Rollers* game. Whether the spin of a wheel or the roll of the dice, what I was doing and becoming was often just a crap shoot. Fortune favors the smart and swift, sure, but I was learning that sometimes winning is just about pure, dumb luck, no matter how cute the shoes I am wearing or how big and tall the foe I am facing.

Put Yourself in My Shoes
You must be present to win.
RB

I sat with a young woman the other day who told me she had been so busy all summer worrying about a job offer that she didn't remember anything about her internship. She said, "I got lost in the plot."

I love that.

First of all, she is way smarter than I was at that age to even consider and reflect on her loss of presence. Way ahead of most of us, I think. Secondly, to give it the slant of story line, to look at her life as a beginning, middle, end plot is singular. How many of us realize we are writing our story daily, and as Annie Dillard says, "How we spend our days, of course, is how we spend our lives."

No matter your particular plot, lay of the land, or storyline, if you do not show up, notice and hold, if not keep some of the plot lines in your heart and heed them—when the game is over, no matter the game—you lose.

What if you stopped looking back to where you've failed or at what games you lost, and instead try to honor where your feet are planted?

What if instead of always looking at what you're doing next, busying your mind with activity after activity, goal after goal, you took a minute to feel proud about the ground you're standing on?

- Life is about being present. It's about relishing where you are and what you have and taking note of what's around you. It's about celebrating, breathing, being, rather than always searching for the next thing, the next item or person you can defeat or find to fill your emptiness.
- Life is about absorbing. About feeling. About existing. About finding where you fit and appreciating the way your life unfolds, on both good and bad days.
- Life is about slowing down. Being still. Finding your place in the universe and being OK with that place, even when it's frustrating, exhausting, beautiful, confusing, or televised on a national game show.

The stakes are high in the game of life. Quit looking back, looking up, looking ahead. Become a high roller. Don't play small with experiences and opportunities. That way, no matter what happens, you win!

Chapter Nine

Goldilocks and the Three Pairs

Life isn't a fairy tale. If you lose your shoes at midnight, chances are you're going to walk home barefoot.

—Factory Outlet shoe ad

I couldn't decide between a "Surfin' Safari" with The Beach Boys drummer Dennis Wilson or holding hands with Paul McCartney as we strolled through London but in the end, it was Davy Jones of The Monkees that I would marry.

None of this actually happened, sadly, but my imaginary boyfriends made it pretty tough for any real guy to compete.

Who could possibly follow that line-up of cute, talented, and rich day-dream dates?

No one.

It's not that I didn't try. But each living, breathing boy was such a disappointment. Watching them on a playground in elementary school, rolling in dirt, slapping each other or hanging from monkey bars only solidified my distress.

'This is what we get to choose from?' I contemplated, sadly.

Instead of singing, they spit. Rather than write songs, they asked for homework help. And there were no surfin' safaris, only Slurpees at 7-Eleven stores. Not to mention that holding hands usually became holding hands back.

I was hoping for a guy who might say, "Your personality is smokin'. I just want to sit you down in a chair and have a lengthy conversation with you." This, of course, was a bigger fairy tale than Dennis, Paul, or Davy.

It was no wonder I was wary of boys and relationships and something called "sex". My dad had shoe-horned in as little information as possible during his rendition of the facts of life. The actual details were a bit hazy, but I got the basics. It went something like, "boys are as scared as you are…but they are made differently and will try to do things and it's up to you to tell them to stop. Most of them will be glad you say no."

What exactly I was supposed to say "no" to and what I had to stop was never explained, so I just kept saying "no" and "stop" to everything.

"Hello!"

"No!"

"Can I help you carry all that stuff?"

"No!"

"Would you like to go get some lunch?"

"No."

"Come on, loosen up and have some fun."

"Stop."

In addition, before my enlightening talk with my dad, my high school Girl Scout troop leader told our entire pack that "boys will drop you like a hot potato if you aren't a virgin."

I was unaware of the VIRGIN merit badge and thought it sounded like a crucial addition to my sash. I wondered what the requirements were.

As if my anatomy lessons and emotional intelligence weren't backward enough, during my freshman year in college every girl in my dorm was reading *The Total Woman*. That little guide explained that men wore the pants and women should greet them wearing nothing but an apron when they came home from work. This sounded a bit one sided, to say the least, and a bit ridiculous, to be sure, but my roommate and others felt it their duty to convince me that this "pleasing" of men was the only way to keep them. The idea that intelligent young women were willing to couple with men that needed to be kept and liked women best naked, stripped me of any interest in dating.

One night an upperclassman from one of my classes named Tony actually came to my dorm room to "have a talk" with me. I thought he wanted to discuss homework.

"The rumor is you are a virgin," he said solemnly and trying to muster sincerity.

"There's a rumor? That's the rumor? About me?"

I was far from shocked to hear that this is what boys talk about. We girls were still on "cute", "hiking boots are hot", and "he looks like he works out." Not once did any girl I knew talk about "is he or is he not?" stuff.

"Now is the time," Tony continued, "college is for experimentation and enjoyment, and your first time should be good." He was now repulsively bovine looking, wide-eyed and attempting to be oh so compassionate to the poor, lonely virgin...I spotted little drips of saliva building up on the sides of his mouth.

"So, why, exactly, are you telling me this?" I asked, dripping too, but with disgust, not desire. It was becoming more clear than ever what 'Boys will be boys' meant.

"I want to volunteer," Tony mooed.

"Volunteer?"

"Yes, I want to be your first. I am qualified, I sort of care about you, I will be gentle, and I think you will like it." He sat back in the chair, crossed his arms in front of his chest, and awaited what he must have thought would be an orgasmic release of thanks and gratitude for his generosity.

I have not been speechless too many times in my life, but I was coming up blank as I stared back at him, seeing him in my mind's eye in sixth grade rolling around in the dirt and picking his nose.

After staring for what seemed a very long time, but what was probably ten seconds, I slowly got up, walked the two tiny steps to my dorm room door, opened it and said,

"Goodbye, Tony."

"You don't even want to consider it? Talk about it?"

I had to hand it to him, Tony was confident. He was calm and clearly sympathetic about my failure to grasp the significance of his generous offer and self sacrifice as he walked out the door.

Two days later a rumor got back to me that Tony and I had slept together.

My dad had explicitly told me he was sending me to college to marry a better level of person than if I didn't go. I was trying to figure out who I was, where I belonged, and in the process look for a man to marry. I felt lost, like Goldilocks, stuck in a deep dark wood far away from home and looking for someone to feed me, shelter me, and keep me safe.

I chose an All-American, ski patrol working, long haired, happy faced boy who was one year ahead of me in college. He was honest, clean, industrious, and fun. One winter morning I looked out from my dorm window, and there in letters six feet high made with footprints etched through the snow on the basketball courts, it said, "I LOVE RONDA."

'I could marry a boy like that' I thought. And I did.

The first pair of wedding shoes were white satin low heels and I walked down the aisle on my dad's arm, ready to play wife and mother way before knowing who I was as a woman. He was a good husband, loyal and kind. I was an imposter, unsure about love, about life, about myself.

I have shined and buffed and re-souled this experience, the ill-fitting, pinched, wrong size excuses, but bottom line is, I failed. I was Goldilocks wearing devoted, committed, vow keeping adult shoes that were just too big for me.

Some women kiss a lot of frogs, or lizards, snakes, and chameleons. I had to go through many different shoes to find the right fit. Musicians, athletes, businessmen, handsome sometimes, cute often, smart occasionally, TV reporters, doctors, construction workers, and destructive, wounded babies in big bodies. Suffice it to say my choice of shoes outshined my choice in men.

Academic achievement or career success offer no vaccine for making mistakes and missteps.

The next pair of shoes was a romp down the aisle in black sequined high heels with a bow in back. He was handsome, with a sports car and I was the breadwinner building a career. I had reason to believe this model might be sustainable.

When my dad arrived home from work, my mom, wearing fresh make-up (and clothes, thank gawd) always greeted him with a cocktail and the newspaper. He sat down sipped and scanned while she made dinner, set the table, got him another drink. I watched this ritual play out night after night and thought, 'when I grow up, I want one of those' meaning a maid, a servant, someone who stayed home and took care of the domestic stuff while I got to wear nice clothes, go out to lunch, and then have dinner waiting for me when my long, tough day was over.

Mr. Sports Car was perfect for the supporting role, I thought. Affable, amenable to taking direction, and zero ambition. But, as it turned out, zero help. Not only did I win the bread, I had to bake it, serve it, and clean up the crumbs. This guy was in it for fun, I needed someone functional.

The black sequined high heels were perfect for a party, but way too small for my everyday groove.

So far, I had satin-shoe boxed myself into a traditional role that was too big and shelved the attempt at an unorthodox black sequined high heel life that was too small

What would you call a woman who's been married twice before she's 30? Impulsive? Opportunistic? Unlucky? Careless? Optimistic? Brave? A hopeless romantic?

My dad asked me if I was a tart.

And then, right in the middle of my wondering and wandering life, love gave me a fairy tale. Someone walked into my life and I knew why it never worked out with anyone else. Everything I thought I knew about love and relationships was suddenly turned on its head.

In relationships before my now husband, I knew what it was like to feel momentarily excited (or even happy) for a little bit. Despite that, I still didn't know what it meant to have a joyful, happy feeling all the time, almost at every single second.

The type of happy I felt wasn't based on the ups and downs of the rest of the world, but instead, was based on knowing I'd found a great partner for life.

I forgot that love should come naturally. I shouldn't have to force it, shouldn't have to put expectations or rules on it, shouldn't have to demand that it happens at a certain time or in a certain way.

I forgot that love isn't about asking someone to change or having someone demand that I be someone different.

I forgot that I shouldn't be searching for perfection, that I shouldn't be holding people to unreachable standards, but instead find someone whose laughter makes me laugh, whose smile turns my frown, whose hands make mine tingle, whose happiness brings light to my life—and loving him because it's really just that simple.

Because the pieces fit.

Because I don't have rules or expectations, but take things day by day, learning who I am alongside another person. Learning that love doesn't have to be so hard. Learning that there will be hard times, fights, pain, and brokenness, but ultimately, things fit together.

I married my husband wearing no shoes. I was barefoot, in the sand. Completely free. At last, I didn't need to hide my feet or my feelings. I waded into the waves with him, feeling beautiful, loved, cherished, and whole. I felt just right.

I have been married now for thirty years. I've come to see that a marriage, based on real, lasting love, is not at all about "living happily ever after." In truth, it is more like a series of challenges that take me deeper into the heart of love.

I like Goldilocks because she was fussy and took what she needed. The missteps I have taken have been necessary to teach me not to settle for things in my life and end up with regrets. Unlike Goldilocks, I learned not to run away if my life or love gets too hot, or too cold, too uncomfortable, too big, or too small. I can and do choose to live happily ever after. To make things as "just right" as I can. Shoes or no shoes.

Put Yourself in My Shoes
Success is a small step taken right now.
RB

Have you ever asked yourself the "why" behind the reason you may stop yourself from starting anything, from stepping into what you really are passionate about doing, from getting out there to create what you want, or discovering who you want to meet and going after it, all because you may not get it just right?

Why have you chosen to believe that failure, a mistake, a misstep, is the other end of success? Could failing and not getting it right help you get one step closer to what you do want and toward what you have set out to do?

It's time to ask yourself why you choose to empower the word failure instead of empowering yourself.

Today you can start redefining what words mean to you versus what someone may have told you. Or believing the story you tell yourself about what failure is. Taking on someone else's belief system and allowing it to disempower you is guaranteed to defeat your feats. You can and should be the author of your story, your fable, your future.

The only way you can ultimately succeed is to fail. To have that misstep. Many women that I coach are asked to define for themselves "failure."

Maybe today is the day for you to revisit it and redefine it.

To decide—ahead of time—the choice to have a different relationship with that misstep when it comes.

Can you see failure in a different way?

Without failing you won't know what to do differently.

And after all, wouldn't you like to know what NOT to do when the "next time" appears?

So, START FAILING. Start not getting it right.

Embrace your missteps every single day until you figure out your road to success; until your job, life, and/or love is more than good enough. Because YOU are already more than good enough.

Find Your Perfect Fit

Stand in the shoes. Press gently on the top of the shoe to make sure you have about a half-inch of space between your longest toe and the end of the shoe. This provides enough room for your foot to press forward as you walk. Wiggle your toes to make sure there's enough room.

> *If you pick someone who cannot or will not give you: space, encourage you to grow, and delight in the ways you need to move forward—you need to reconsider, it's definitely an ill-fit.*

Walk around in the shoes to determine how they feel. Is there enough room at the balls of the feet? Do the heels fit snugly, or do they pinch, rub, or slip off? Don't rationalize that the shoes just need to be "broken in." Find shoes that fit from the start.

> *Too many of us make ourselves small, or quiet, or unopinionated in order to fit with someone. If you do this from the beginning, if you lie on your dating profile or on your first dinner date, you will have to keep this pretend perfect fit up forever. Thinking that someone just needs time to be broken in results in breaking up or breaking apart.*

Trust your own comfort level rather than a shoe's size or description. Sizes vary between manufacturers. And no matter how comfortable an advertisement claims those shoes are, you're the real judge.

Your friends like him, your parents think she's the one, but when you wear the idea, you feel squeezed, constricted, or concerned. Do not buy into what others think is good for you. You'll end up limping through life. No one walks in your shoes, except you.

Pay attention to width as well as length. If the ball of your foot feels compressed in a particular shoe, ask if it comes in a wider size.

Life should be deep and wide, filled with variety and velocity. If you are a hiking boot and she is stilettos, or you are running shoes and he is loafers, make sure you can adjust and appreciate the narrowing this may cause during years of wear and tear.

Examine the soles. Are they sturdy enough to provide protection from sharp objects? Do they provide any cushioning? Take note of how they feel as you walk around the shoe store. Try to walk on hard surfaces as well as carpet to see how the shoe feels on both.

Is she beautiful? Is he handsome? Rich? Blonde? Muscular? A fit based on the visible and material while not considering the sturdiness and adaptability of the soul is a sure formula for emotional blisters and coming apart at the seams. A good soul can soften the hard surfaces you are bound to step on.

Chapter Ten

One Two Buckle My Shoe

The only things kids wear out faster than shoes is their parents.

—John J. Plomp

"I think that might be your sphincter muscle on the table."

Giving birth is one test I couldn't really study for; I was prepared for most of the scenarios, but I couldn't know everything that was going to be on the quiz. Or the delivery table.

I read lots of articles and was told by well meaning people what a special time being pregnant would be. They extolled the rosy glow I would get, but failed to mention the way my butt and hips would meld into one. Or the fact that just rolling over in bed would become a three-part miniseries on Netflix. No one ever, ever, mentioned hemorrhoids or inverted nipples.

Not that I didn't enjoy some perks, like when people asked me, "What did you do today?" I could say "I made ears." Or if my husband asked me to run an errand I could complain and shriek, "I made a hand today, what the heck have you done?"

The reason I found myself ready to give birth and sixty pounds heavier—eating Mystic Mint cookies for breakfast and floating all summer in a pool wearing a black and white maternity swimsuit and looking like Sea World's killer whale Shamu—was, as so many things in my life were, directly related to a conversation with my dad. And, to be fair, a Betsy Wetsy doll.

Betsy was the most popular doll of the era. But her market appeal had nothing to do with her golden locks, bright blue eyes, gingham dress, or white baby booties. Her selling point was she cried real tears, needed bathing, and wet her pants when I gave her a bottle of water. And then I got to change her diaper! Oodles of fun! What little girl wouldn't want a Betsy Wetsy? I could be a more than a little girl, I could be an instant Mommy, too.

Which is precisely what my dad was saying to me at lunch one afternoon prior to my even considering having children. The maître d' escorted me to a corner table where my dad was seated and sipping a long, tall gin and tonic. "Hello Daddy," I said loud enough to make sure everyone within earshot knew this was my father not my date. I was always deathly afraid that with less than two decades between us and living in LA, anyone would assume, God forbid, that I was his girlfriend.

He bypassed any pleasantries and got right to the topic of the day after I ordered a Coke.

He was concerned that I had been married almost six months and wasn't pregnant. He began to wax poetically about the wonder and value of having your own children. He asked me to think about my poor Aunt Inie who was childless.

"Who do you think will take care of her when she is old?" he asked.

I was staring at him, possible responses buzzing through my brain like a beehive that had been knocked over. Truth be told I immediately wondered how many gin and tonics he might have had before I arrived. He was suddenly waxing poetic about parenting?

This was the same father, the same parent, that called my brother pinhead. Who told me my rear end was two axe handles wide. The man who wanted us to speak only when spoken to and ask "how high?" when asked to jump. The same parent forced into marriage by an unwanted pregnancy. 'Now, *now* he's a fan of family?' I thought.

"Gee, Daddy, maybe Uncle John will take care of Aunt Inie, or she could live with a group of friends in a commune."

"Ronda, how sad is that? She will be all alone, with no one who cares, who loves her, no child to visit…" he looked so concerned all of a sudden for Aunt Inie, his mother's sister, who he visited maybe twice a year, even though she had been instrumental and included throughout his childhood.

"Well, I guess Aunt Inie must have wanted it this way. Besides, they have homes especially for old people, that's where most kids put their parents anyway," I added brightly, "not to mention our current population boom, there are too many people on this planet already." I sipped my Coke and felt smug, congratulating myself with an 'impregnable point to Ronda!' I think my self satisfied and righteous head even bobbled.

And then, he pulled out all the stops necessary for the daughter of a narcissist—who is desperate for approval—to fold, crumble, and melt into the floor like the Wicked Witch of the West who preferred flying monkeys to having children.

"You're right, there are a lot of people and a lot of problems, but what if Abraham Lincoln's mother had decided not to have children? What if Mahatma Gandhi's mother said, 'Nope, too many people already?'"

I was bracing for a tale of Jesus' mother when he continued, "How do you know your child, your children, will not be the one to change things? To make the world better? To solve hunger or create better laws? How can you be sure a child of yours will not be the one to invent or devise or deliver a way to help mankind?"

And then, the close of this pitch came swift, heavy, and right to my heart.

"And if anyone should be a mother, it is you. You are smart, creative, fun, and talented; you will be a wonderful mother and your children will be so lucky."

Here I was again, sitting with my dad, hanging on every word like I did on that sunny afternoon by the pool when he told me my feet were ugly. I knew that once more the direction of my footprints was going to be forever altered by the bottomless pit of need for his acknowledgement of my worth. A need I could not, evidently, ever drown out.

The concept that a child of mine could make the world better, maybe even become another Abe Lincoln was heady stuff. And being told I would be good at it? Less than a month after the gin and tonic lunch, I was pregnant with my little world changer and standing in my kitchen with a container of Drano.

When I was pregnant, there were no standard ultrasounds, no way to find out if I was having a boy or girl. But I had read in a woman's magazine about a foolproof, at home method that promised to result in knowing the gender of your unborn Mahatma. By adding urine to Drano, the stuff that gets poured down a clogged drain to break up whatever hair, grease, and other detritus that is preventing drainage, the resulting blue chemical reaction meant boy and no color meant girl.

I pulled out the Drano I purchased for this experiment, fluffed a good amount of the crystals into a tall ice tea glass, added fresh pee I collected in a kitchen measuring cup, and stood aside waiting to see if I was giving birth to another Mother Teresa or the next President of the United States.

The magazine article did not specify amounts, so I had filled half the glass with Drano and another fourth of the glass with urine, leaving just enough room at the top of the glass for the color, and hence gender, to be revealed. 'Like the slogan says,' I thought, dizzy with anticipation, 'this is a better life through chemistry.'

The filled glass started to shake—like earthquake kind of shake—the Drano and pee were fizzing, whizzing, foaming, and gurgling up, up, up, with fumes whirling around the kitchen and the smell…the smell was a combination of toxic dump, fingernails burning, human flesh searing, and rotting blue cheese smell. Within moments the house was filled with Drano fog. I could barely breathe.

I had to leave the house quickly and ended up spending the afternoon at a neighbor's while my house aired out. I recalled that my chemistry grade in college did bring my GPA down.

With all the foaming and rumbling, I couldn't even see any color. I would have to wait months to know if it was a boy or girl. In addition, I became seriously worried about possible damage done to my unknown planetary hero by the chemical fumes that I had inhaled.

That day is when the idea of being someone's mother clicked for me.

'I am *supposed* to change. I am *supposed* to be a better version of my current self. I am *supposed* to feel different. I am *supposed* to grow and evolve. I am *supposed* to think of someone's else's safety, benefit, and care.' Being a mother was what was needed to drain me of selfishness and stupidity.

True, I was off to a shaky start, but I was grateful I had nine months to improve not just myself, but my domestic choices.

My shoe choices also needed improving. It didn't take me long to discover my shoes had to be slip-ons. Good-bye, for awhile, to high heels because of swollen ankles, and farewell to any shoe with laces. I never wore shoes with laces. Because once my bump got big enough, I couldn't bend over to tie them.

My baby's first kicks felt like a tap-tap-tap morse code message from the luxury stateroom in the middle of his or her amniotic ocean liner. This messaging was the start of the most intimate conversation I'd ever had. Being pregnant is the ultimate intimacy possible between human beings. I think it may be a vehicle meant to awaken more love within women and bring more love into the world. That's what happened to me, anyway. I was in love, big time, with everything and everyone. Except maybe BBQ chicken. I was pure euphoria…mixed with nauseous.

I read in another women's magazine that your baby can hear you and will know it's your voice once out of the womb. That was all I needed to embark on a thirty-six-week monologue. I kept talking almost non-stop and with no interruptions.

I told him or her all about me, what I hoped for us together and what a good mother I would try to be everyday for the rest of my life. I told my baby stories of my childhood, stories of my feats, and I promised to dedicate myself to assist his or her chosen feats as well as help turn any defeats into lessons not liabilities. I would, I told my baby, teach how to tie or buckle shoes and untangle issues.

I read my in-utero baby fairy tales and my favorite rhymes.

I told jokes, I sang songs, I described trees and the sky, and I asked him or her to kick in on name choices. Two kicks if it was a good name, one hard kick if not.

My last face to fetus conversation was,

"Now? In the middle of the night?" as I rushed to the bathroom just in time for my water to break all over tile instead of carpet. "You're a thoughtful person already," I said. "OK, let's do this."

The details of my three-hour labor for my almost ten-pound baby are hazy. I remember my private parts being shaved, an enema administered, and hearing that my sphincter muscle plopped out right after my son did. I remember his quiet "waaa" and straining to see if he was Drano damaged.

I remember his father saying to the nurse, "My shoulders are so sore from holding her up all the times she pushed," while I was receiving sixteen vaginal stitches. Just as I was about to leap off the table with a needle and thread hanging from my crotch and slug him the doctor announced,

"A big, healthy baby boy!" and brought him to me.

Thanks to a narrow birth canal, he looked a little like King Tut, his head was pointed, and his face was ruddy, but he was one hundred percent healthy. I opened my arms and held him for the first time. He was fidgety and quietly whimpering and then, it happened. I said, "Hello handsome." The moment he heard my voice, his body relaxed, and he began blinking and straining to focus on the face of the voice he knew. His mother's voice. My voice.

I was a goner. And I was, after non-stop chattering for nine months, reverently quiet. The emotions I had yet to express, the speeches I had yet to deliver about birds and bees, homework, drugs, and girls, the years and years of conversations ahead of us would have to wait. For this moment all I could manage was a little humming with a big lump in my throat.

I have found motherhood to be the deepest well of mattering, even while experiencing the hardest trials of my life. I have learned to rise to any occasion and have found myself lifted to new heights, while stretching beyond any and all limits I once put upon myself. With rarely a dull moment, I've experienced more adventure in mothering than ever imaginable.

Motherhood gives me an excuse to stay young forever, to kick off my shoes and let down my hair while enjoying love beyond measure.

So, I have to hand it to my dad, he was right on this one. My children did change the world, the world as I knew it. The world became a better, more loving, and hope full place. And being their mother is my life, my joy, my passion, my greatest feat.

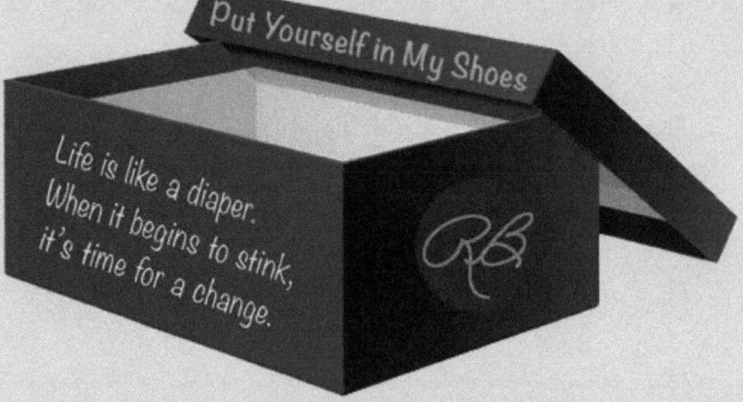

Change comes in many forms. Change can be moving, having children, getting or losing a job, getting married, getting divorced, losing a loved one, or just picking a different menu item at your favorite restaurant. And everyone fears change. People who say they don't are either lying to you or themselves.

Without change, there would no longer be any beauty in the world. Flowers would stop blooming, the leaves would stop changing colors and falling, fruits and vegetables would no longer grow, animals would no longer have cute little babies, and homes would never be built. What is here now would be the same; forever. You'd be changing the same diapers, working on the same project, and sitting in the same chair at the same house forever. Eek!

Don't wait for your dad, your friend, your defeats, or wins to insist you change. Don't wait until your life well and truly sucks before paying attention to the signs that it's time for a change.

Think of it this way, change is simply growing. When we are born, we are little and we know little. As we change and grow, we become new people. We change, we adapt, and continue to grow. Without change we cannot grow; we become stagnant. We like different people, different music, different books, and different television shows as the years go by. We change from liking cartoons to liking adult comedies. We change from listening to our parents to being parents ourselves.

The only fear we should have when it comes to change is that change will stop happening. If change stops, we stop. We will no longer grow. We will never become more. We may as well stop living.

Having children changed my shoes as well as my life. It wasn't always for the best or most pleasant. I missed my red high heels and I wish I could have missed out on stinky diapers. My life got a little more hectic, busy, and complicated. But more importantly, the changes made me better in more ways than I can count.

From now on, try thinking of yourself as a "game-changer". Have you noticed how that that term always means something is about to improve? It will never be easy, but once you've stepped outside of your comfort zone and on to greater things, you will thank your "past self" for making the life-changing decision of embracing change. You will give birth to new opportunities, new ideas, and new talents. And the stretch marks will be invisible because they are in your brain and on your heart.

Chapter Eleven

Espadrilles are French, Oui?

To wear dreams on one's feet is to begin
to give a reality to one's dreams.

—Roger Vivier

I invented virtual reality at my dinner table.

I am not claiming I created the goggle wearing, arm waving, lost in space virtual reality, but rather I was an early and forced adapter of the have no money, live in a small town, want to show my children the world version of virtual reality.

With me as their mother, my sons may rightfully claim their entire childhood was an experience in augmented reality. We did lunchtime opera, singing arias about peanut butter sandwiches. We planted the sesame seeds from fast food hamburger buns in hopes that little burgers would sprout. Before Sunday morning waffles we did family workouts running upstairs, crawling under beds, or lifting heavy laundry baskets to find and follow commands on index cards like 10 JUMPING

JACKS or 15 PUSH-UPS strewn all around the house with the theme from the movie Rocky blasting from my Radio Shack plastic turntable and cheap speakers.

Being a mom was an unexpected but deeply appreciated reminder of what is most worthwhile about life. I could choose to celebrate and innovate during the challenges or find the daily grind irritating and aggravating. Therefore, we didn't just grocery shop, we did a treasure hunt. "Who can find sharp cheddar cheese?" Why just watch a movie when we could turn down the sound and become screenwriters? Motherhood was a chance to bake the best un-birthday cake ever made. Dinner is not tuna on English muffins, it's tuna boats!

Seeing life through my kids' eyes gave me the opportunity to revisit my own childhood and create a new reality full of hope, purpose, adventure—in other words, creating what I wanted from my childhood and sharing it.

Being a parent stirred me to put myself in my children's shoes at the same time that I put myself in my own young self's shoes. Like most parents, I wanted to give my kids the world—a creative, crazy, loving, unusual, and interesting-people populated, and joyful world.

One Sunday morning, my youngest son walked in holding the magazine section of the paper and almost demanded we enter a contest.

"Mom," he said, handing me the *Parade* supplement, "Look at this, this is most definitely us!"

The headline he pointed to read, "ARE YOU AMERICA'S MOST CREATIVE FAMILY?"

"Mom, we are the MOST creative, you know we are, we do stuff no one does, none of my friends do, this is really us, let's enter, I know we will win!" He was jumping up and down.

His wide-eyed, flushed face, his infectious enthusiasm and certainty that we had a winning family was all the prize I needed.

OK.

Busted.

Being a mother didn't change my essence, I did think it would be a fun feat for my family. I could imagine us on the cover of Parade and making an appearance on the local, maybe national news. I could picture my kids being proud of their family. Most importantly, I could visualize us with the prize money. So, we entered the national search for America's Most Creative Family.

We had to submit a less than 500-word essay that described some activity that brought family members together, promoted bonding, and was original and inventive.

Promote bonding? We did weekly Friday night family skits—like my favorite "YOU BE THE MIME" produced, written, and performed by my sons. All the lights in the living room were turned low as my husband and I entered when given the OK. A Marcel Marceau lookalike, who looked more like my son, took the hand drawn tickets we had been issued earlier that day in exchange for a stack of cards with phrases and/or single nouns printed on them. The white face was leftover makeup from Halloween, my lipstick had been amply utilized, and upon closer examination the suspenders were old belts hooked inside their jeans. The black stripes on their shirts, part and parcel of all good mime apparel, were simply lines colored in with a felt tip marker. Not a word was spoken, even in the introduction, as both of them acted out how to pick a card and then mime the word or phrase we had been given.

Original? One Saturday morning as I was leaving for the grocery store, my sons ran to catch me and give me a "gift."

"Here's some music we made for you," said the youngest boy.

"Yeah, Mom," chimed in the eldest, "It will make your chores more fun, you can even use it for a workout tape." Their little, sweet faces were beaming up at me.

"You made me a playlist?" I choked up, so touched by the thoughtful gesture from my young, innocent, and kind sons. Who else in the world had boys like this, who else could boast of the thoughtfulness, kindness, and generosity?

I kissed them both, thought about the ice cream I would bring home as a thank you, and got into my car. I put the precious tape into the player and pushed play as I backed out of the garage. I was bopping along to a well-chosen Marvin Gaye song from boys who really knew me, valued me, and loved me when abruptly the Marvin Gaye song was stopped mid-chorus with my youngest saying, "raise your son's allowance, raise your son's allowance." The song started back up and within 45 seconds another 'hidden message' played, "buy some ice cream for your sons, buy some ice cream for your sons." These hidden persuasion alerts were scattered throughout the thoughtful "gift" cassette! When I got home, I said,

"I don't know why, but I just had the feeling you guys would like some ice cream today." The look on their faces as they shot a wide-eyed look at each other! They were sure the subliminal approach had worked its magic.

I didn't raise their allowance, hoping I might get another attempt and cassette.

Inventive? We pulled out all the stops for our annual family viewing of the Oscars. Using only what we had in our closets, the challenge was to dress like one of the characters or a star in a nominated, or we thought should be nominated, movie. My favorite year was my husband sporting a beard he drew on his face with shoe polish, tank top and jeans, holding a bike chain channeling *Dead Man Walking*. My youngest son dressed in a suit with a swastika emblem he had drawn on paper to pin to his lapel portraying Oskar Schindler from *Schindler's List*. My other son donned a striped towel, shorts, and a blue crème clay mask—meant for nourishing dry skin—plastered all over his face calling out "FREEDOM" because he was Mel Gibson in *Braveheart*! I pull out all the fancy wedding gift silver and prepare appetizers, we drink champagne and sparkling cider from crystal flutes and party like all the A-listers.

After a lively back and forth with the family, as well as lots of laughs, we hit upon what we thought would put us in the running for America's Most Creative Family.

And that idea was getting out of America.

I had continually chosen small university towns in which to live. Places like Lubbock, Texas, Shippensburg, Pennsylvania, and now Flagstaff, Arizona. These places were manageable, friendly, safe, and fulfilled my long-standing I want to be a Walton dream.

My family of origin made such fun of me watching *The Waltons* or similar family-loves-each-other-and-conquers-adversities-together-that-only-deepens-their-bonds shows. They called me a sap.

Sap that I was, when I had my own family, I desired and designed to have that warmth, togetherness, open space, and "Good night John-Boy" feeling. I believed small towns would provide the best backdrop for the sentimental *Wonder Years* type of environment I wanted to provide.

One of the drawbacks of my choice to live in a small town was a creeping and discernible *Bonanza* type ethnocentrism. Meaning my sons—like the Cartwright and Walton families—were parochial regarding the world at large; growing increasingly unfamiliar with other viewpoints, foods, and cultures.

To counterbalance the Disneyland "It's a Small World" syndrome, I pioneered the virtual and augmented reality approach to life at our home.

I took my sons everywhere and anywhere I went—whether teaching college courses, celebrations at fraternities and sororities, judging Greek life lip synching or step competitions, choir performances, faculty recitals, homecoming parades, lectures from visiting faculty; basically, everything a university town and college professor job allows. My boys had education majors as babysitters. Pretty sorority sisters who cuddled them. Their immediate world was filled and fulfilling, but other continents and the manner and experience of an overseas locale or foreign family life was non-existent. As was my bank account. Our "trips" consisted of outings to bookstores, daytrips, concerts, and the foreign movie house in our town. And, I was not exactly a well-seasoned traveler myself, unless you count college beer runs in British Columbia and cheap sandal shopping in Tijuana.

Wanting my sons to be at home in the world and see global possibilities for themselves was why I created a monthly International Dinner Party.

Each month we picked a different country to visit virtually, never leaving our dining room. I would go to our neighborhood travel agent and get posters for our destination that month and cook food with recipes garnered from the *Betty Crocker International Cookbook*. The boys had to research the history, culture, and language of our chosen place and devise local street art drawings, placemats or signs, and write music to play on our piano that sounded, to them, authentic. The most fun became designing and costuming ourselves as a native of the country we picked—without spending money. In other words, from searching through closets, we dressed like a person from, say, Mexico would dress. Or so we imagined, guessed, goofed, and made do.

Our first country of choice was Japan.

Ramen, Yakitori, and rice recipes, plus a red kimono my dad had brought back from his trip to Kyoto and I was ready.

The boys drew cherry blossoms on paper placemats and unveiled their customary dress, one at a time.

My oldest son dressed like his concept of a Japanese tourist—complete with baseball hat and a camera hanging from his neck.

My youngest son appeared in his only suit, a small black ribbon tied in a bow under his collar, and a small goatee and mustache drawn on with my eyeliner pencil.

We stood and stared for a moment, trying to figure his interpretation out, when he blurted, "I'm Charlie Chan!"

We virtually visited and dined in cities throughout Africa, South America, Europe, and Asia. These dinners were what we chose to describe in our 500-word essay entry to be America's Most Creative Family and, like my son predicted, we won first place!

USA Today sent a photographer and journalist to follow us step-by-step through one of our country visits. We chose France and I had quite the argument on my hands when I told the boys french fries would not be on the menu. Wearing newsboy caps backward and at an angle, they fashioned berets. They learned the song "Les Poissons" from *The Little Mermaid* and made cherry clafouti for dessert.

For dinner we had mushroom crepes with French style green beans. Scouring my closet for my French outfit, I found a flowered dress, a big hat with a sunflower right in the middle, and espadrilles! Truthfully, I didn't know or call them espadrilles until I needed to be a French girl, but they were canvas, rope heeled, and voila!

We drank sparkling cider from champagne flutes and felt like celebrities as the flash bulbs kept popping to capture America's Most Creative Family's evening in Paris.

The prize money was enough to virtually pay for a real trip to Europe. We threw frisbees in Hyde Park, lit candles in Notre

Dame, devoured waffles in Bruges, and climbed the steep stairs that lead to castles in Germany. It was a once in a lifetime experience that we shared and it proved what I already suspected, your whole world is really at your dinner table, no matter where you put your slippers at night.

Put Yourself in My Shoes
It doesn't matter how great your shoes are if you don't accomplish anything in them.
—Martina Boone
RB

Our virtual journey around the world, our time doing skits, reading plays, the costumes, the cacophony, the characters, and the creativity should not have won a prize. What we did and how we did it is something everyone could do, cost little time and no money, and made our family bonds strong, our children confident, and our memories meaningful.

To quote psychologist Abraham Maslow, "The key question isn't 'What fosters creativity?' But why in God's name isn't everyone creative? Where was the human potential lost? How was it crippled? I think therefore a good question might be not why do people create? But why do people not create or innovate?"

Creativity is about more than self-expression; it's about learning, process, and mastery. It's about coming up with ideas, lots of little ideas that add up to big bold ideas that just might change your life, or the world. Or—enable you to see the world.

A creative life is all about working from that sweet spot where your gifts and the world intersect, where what you do has fascination and relevance. It's about doing something close to your soul, and sharing that with the world, or the people in your living room.

Creativity helps build healthy intrapersonal and interpersonal relationships. So, whether you are a parent, an athlete, a doctor, or a retiree, make sure that this is one area of your life that you frequently evoke. I bet every chore you have, challenge you face, and meal you eat could use a creative overhaul. Have fun, make a mess, be an amateur. Take it from the winner of America's Most Creative Family, what have you got to lose?

Chapter Twelve

Schooled Shoes

Don't try to squeeze into a glass slipper.
Instead, shatter the glass ceiling.

—Priyanka Chopra

I want to be The Crocodile Hunter, with tenure.

The overheated, university auditorium is filled to capacity, almost four hundred undergraduate education majors are in the room to begin their careers as teachers, coaches, band directors, or principals. The smell of anxiety coupled with the excitement that comes with hope permeates the room as Pink Floyd's, "We don't need no education, we don't need no thought control…" blares from the cheap sound system. The students are wide-eyed and wary; and probably wondering who Pink Floyd is.

I stomp onto the stage wearing high top hiking boots, a pith helmet, khaki shorts, and a matching safari shirt. I am trying to look as much like Steve Irwin, the real Crocodile Hunter, as I can, given my budget and gender. I tip-toe toward an inflated, plastic, but menacing, pool-toy crocodile being pulled little by little by a string by one of my teaching assistants who is hidden in the wings. Now the theme from the movie "Jaws" is da-da, da-da, dadadadada-ing throughout the auditorium as the lights go down and a spotlight focuses on me advancing in the direction of the threatening reptile.

"By Crikey, this little beauty in known as Crocodile Functionus Carnivoreus Educationists…he eats mediocre teachers," I shout with all the glee, enthusiasm, and relish Irwin had when he spotted a croc on his television show. "And this beauty never goes hungry, seems there is a surplus of his preferred food."

It's his verve, his eternal elation, his love of the subject matter and sharing it that I am desperately attempting to replicate. I pounce on the pretend reptile and wrestle with it, finally pinning it, and turning toward the stunned students shout, "This is what it's like trying to teach! It's a battle every day, in every way. And you don't always end up on top."

With that I begin an Intro to Education class that will become the most popular and most criticized class on campus. Popular because I tap into what students need, how they feel, what the real fears about becoming a teacher are; and criticized because I spend less time on Horace Greeley, John Dewey, and other historical figures and facts then the school's antiquated curriculum and tenured professors, themselves antiques, demand.

The class is intended to cull those who can from those who can't or shouldn't teach, as well as model effective teaching practice. To that end I have played the part of the host of Survivor wearing flip-flops and an Hawaiian shirt, one of the Backstreet Boys donning leather boots and motorcycle jacket and even Oprah balancing on fake Jimmy Choos in my relentless pursuit of making the class memorable, motivating, and instructional.

I often fall short, but the attempts and adventure, impact and import, self-reliance and self-reflection, for me, make teaching the last great job on earth.

I never entertained the idea of teaching as a career. Never felt "the calling" that so many educators do. My dad told me when I was about thirteen that I would be a good teacher, and that it was a better job than a nurse, which seemed to be his opinion of my options. He told me I was bossy enough and ham enough to pull off teaching; but lacked the empathy and compassion to be a nurse. He was spot on, of course. In our family, if you had empathy, sympathy, compassion, or any soft spot, that is precisely where you would get the old emotional whack. I was interested in neither being a nurse or a teacher. I was in my Monkees—particularly Davy Jones, as my 'destiny-and-purpose-in-life'—phase. Who needed a career when I would be swept off my feet and onto a private plane by a cute millionaire musician for the next concert appearance?

How I began what would eventually become my calling, my vocation, my voice, and my contribution was, as many things that change your life often are, a fluke. Going to grad school for an MBA, I was asked to teach a class in advertising and marketing, for which I would receive free tuition and a stipend. Done Deal.

I prepped my first copywriting class, which was a ninety-minute session. I walked into the classroom looking as professorial as I could. I was carrying a brief case and a regal, arrogant, know-it-all air. I am sure my nose was elevated and my demeanor patrician. I read through my lecture, pausing only occasionally to look at the class members. When I had finished my soliloquy, I looked up at the clock and realized I had sixty minutes left! I had been speed talking, which explained why the students were not taking notes and sat staring at me, with their mouths slightly open. BUT…I loved it. The creativity of preparing a class, the performance aspect, the drama or comedy demanded to be effective, the youth, possibility, spontaneous dance of discussions, as well as the good cheer and energy in the room—not to mention a captive audience. Every single thing that I had ever thought about being or doing was all wrapped up within the four walls of a classroom.

Who knew? I know, my dad.

Standing in that classroom, speaking as quickly as an announcer for a drug ad who has to explain the side effects, I realized that working in advertising, public relations, and television had forced me into some ill-fitting shoes. Shoes that were too tight, some with heels too high, some just plain trying too hard. But when I donned beige and brown wingtips and entered that first classroom as a professor I was, at long last, wearing the right shoe, in the right place, and for the right reason. Those lace up mini-men's shoes provided my glass slipper moment, my opportunity to be Cinderella for a ninety-minute class. I was, at long last, starring in a fairy tale with complete authorship over the story line and utter control over insuring a happy ending.

Like Cinderella, I had ugly stepsisters standing in my path by the name of Time and Money. Pursuing my Ph.D. crown cost me twelve years of my life because I was only able to take one class at a time. I was working full time, parenting more than full time, and driving hours each week to take the required coursework. I taped class lectures on audio cassettes so I could listen and learn on the lonely, long drives to and from my home to the campus. I did my day job, got the kids to school, made dinners, and helped with homework until their bedtime. I prepped for teaching my own five classes, wrote papers, learned statistics from 10:00 p.m.–2:00 a.m., got some sleep, and then started all over again at 5:00 a.m. I was exhausted. I began to schedule time to cry in the shower nightly, overcome by the possibility that this call to teach and game of degrees would never be worth the missed hikes, ball games, and general horsing around with my sons. Thinking about correlations and SES stats while dining with friends, as well as the mental masturbation of most of the social science research I was forced to read and endeavor to produce, was seeping into my generally upbeat personality and making me four out of the seven dwarfs: Sleepy, Grouchy, Dopey, and all only to be Doc.

There were so many times I wanted to quit, times I lost sight and faith…until I entered a classroom to teach, felt all over again the extravagant boundaries of who and what a teacher can do and be, and was revived and renewed…until the next crying jag in the shower.

The doctoral odyssey finally came to an end and my dissertation was selected as the best in the College of Education. I was also named Outstanding Graduate Student. This all paled in comparison to how proud my sons were as they escorted me to the ceremony. I was bedecked in my academic gown, honor cords, Oxford mortarboard, and black heels. Those heels click-clacked across the wooden stage as I strode forward and up to receive my degree. I held the diploma skyward toward my boys sitting in the stands, and shouted, "We did it!"

Armed with the title, Dr. Beaman, I quickly established myself as what I like to call an iconoclast, but my fellow teachers called a kook. I created 24-hour Teach-Ins raising thousands of dollars to build schools in Africa, until the state comptroller told me I could not have a class bank account. My students and I built libraries for local Head Start schools, until the dean told me I could not transport students off campus. I lit tiki torches and had student assistants walk down the aisles with them ablaze to recreate the *Survivor* show, until the fire marshal got wind of my props and shut me down. OK, I understand that one.

With every turn, every pedagogical parlay, I would find myself stymied, threatened, or blocked. I consoled myself with believing prophets are never appreciated in their own time. Turns out being brash, bold, and blonde are not exactly appreciated in the hallowed halls or well received by the stuffed shirts standing in front of hollow classrooms. I often found anonymous typed letters with explicit threats regarding not getting promoted or just plain ugly remarks about my looks in my office mailbox. I once got a Playboy centerfold scrunched into my mailbox with a note attached that said, "This is what students think of you," and when I won a national teaching award my dean came into my office and said, "I wonder if I had nice legs if I would have been named best professor in the country."

Sure, these things hurt and wobbled me, and I worried for my chance of success in my dream job; but, within the closed doors of my classrooms, magic was happening, spells were being cast, and wishes were coming true. I knew teaching was my superpower. I wasn't going to let small minds walking around in Florsheims or Birkenstocks stop me.

Whether donning hiking boots, high heels, sandals, or loafers, my foothold in the academy was tenuous, not tenured. I believed, however, if I did not step forward, no matter what shoes I was are wearing, I would always be in the same place, fighting the same battles and blowhards. I could not, would not, let them stop me in my tracks.

Which is why I accepted the invitation from the university president to be a commencement speaker. I thought it would, at last, give me some cred with my peers. Speaking to an audience of ten thousand, over 2,500 of them students, on one of the few golden moments a human being gets in a lifetime. I was down. In fact, I had another BIG idea and wanted to be rappelled down from the top of the stadium as my entrance. Suffice it to say that when I proposed this, the staring ovation I received by the commencement committee was all I needed to know it was no.

My speech was a Dr. Seuss tour de force. Dressed as The Cat in the Hat, my red high-top sneakers steadied my stroll to the podium, and I commenced to deliver a twelve-minute poem that took the graduates down a four-year memory lane in whimsical rhyme accompanied by guest appearances by the school mascot and an a cappella choir. It was a fun, interactive, yet sentimental and honoring commencement address targeted right toward the hearts and souls of the students and their families.

At the final stanza, the entire audience, students, and their ten thousand guests, rose in unison for a thundering standing ovation that erupted into cheers, yells, and whoops which seemed to last as long as moments like this do in movies. Everyone in the stadium was as ecstatic—waving pom-poms, hats, pennants, and even purses—as if I had made a winning touchdown in a national championship game.

Well, everyone except the faculty sitting down in front of me, below the stage. I saw only hundreds of dour faces and sour grapes. They looked past me or stared at their folded hands positioned on their laps. Some were staring at the ground and all were staying seated in their chairs rather than join in the applause. I was thankful they didn't have tomatoes to throw! The next day I heard that many of them called the president of the university complaining, and I quote, "Commencement should not be entertaining."

My dad once told me nothing succeeds like success. Like my role model, The Crocodile Hunter, I remained dauntless in my pursuit of being a good and true teacher. After years of struggle and ridicule, the tides began to turn. I have been named All University Professor of the year at three institutions, selected as an Outstanding Young Woman in America, and named the first recipient of the NEA Art of Teaching Award. The shoes I wear to teach continue to make a loud and clear clack down the halls. I pass faculty offices peopled by professors who don't greet me but it never dilutes or dismays me. I cannot help but practically leap into the clamor and chaos filled classrooms where the action really is; I am on the hunt for possibility, and ready to attack and tackle ignorance. It's the students who turn my way as I pop in, greeting them as I rush to the front of the room, turn, and say, "Hello, everybody, let's go!"

Their expressions tell me they are anxious to try on a new style, willing to walk into new worlds with me, and "Crikey", they are determined to explore their outer, mid, and inner souls.

The sound of a loud pair of shoes can summon a range of associations for anyone within hearing. Depending on the speed and force of the wearer's walk, these sounds can indicate nerves, authority, anger, or hesitation. They can fill a room with a womanly aura—or a dread. Whether intended or not, these shoes are sure to get whoever is wearing them attention.

In general, research implies that people wear loud shoes because they do want to be noticed. This motivation to be noticed is especially powerful in people who are sometimes regarded as low in prestige or status—like housewives, mothers, daycare workers, and people who are the victims of prejudice or injustice. After people are noticed, they feel more powerful; offsetting the sense of powerlessness that prejudice can evoke.

As a senior in high school, after I got my first office job—at a sales gimmick company called New Method

Enterprises, where I acted as receptionist and shill for pulling unsuspecting people into the office to pick up free soup—I dropped $40 on a pair of wooden, stacked-heel sandals.

In addition to the $4/an hour and driving myself to work, the noise these shoes made as I walked down the office's hardwood floor hallway made me feel like an adult force of nature. Learning to be poised and ladylike as I mastered the trudge of the heavy, wooden sandals was an apt metaphor for being a hopeful but totally unsure 17-year-old getting the hang of feigning composure.

The look of a shoe matters but the sound can empower you. The sound is like 'hey look, hey look, hey look.' And finding a little power can outfit you with the strength to speak up during a presentation, ask for that promotion, take on a bureaucracy, or wink at a cute stranger.

Conversely, a loud shoe can give off a warning. At night, walking to the parking lot in those loud wooden shoes made a co-worker exclaim, "Damn, you walk like you're six feet tall!"

Hiking boots or high heels, it's not all about the shoes. It's about the confidence you have wearing them, the desire to have impact and be heard, and the click clack of someone who knows where she is going and alerts others to get out of her way.

Chapter Thirteen

In My Mother's Shoes

I own one pair of Prada shoes. They make my feet hurt...It's not the shoes' fault; they are exquisitely made. I blame my feet. I've got my mother's feet.

—Meryl Streep

Looking at the CAT scan screen I think, 'The Kardashians and Real Housewives got nothing. This is Reality TV.'

I am blinking fast and furious faucets of tears hoping I can lift off and out of this cramped, over-heated office fueled solely by eyelash power. The young oncologist is calm. The scene, like his job, is a re-run, scripted with words like "cancer," "stage four," "eight months to a year," "so sorry," "do what we can."

The star of this show is my mother, gazing dispassionately at the display of her ravaged insides, deserving of an Emmy for her portrayal of the heroic patient who will triumph.

"I will treat you as if you were my own mother," the doctor says as he puts his arm around her.

"I would rather have you treat me like I was your girlfriend...I think I'll get better care that way," she says as she turns her face upward, leans into his hug, bats her own eyelashes, and smiles.

My mother had played the role of beautiful wife for over fifty years. As a recent widow, now adrift, she committed that day to her metastases as she had her marriage, devoted, singular, brave, and with consistent humor.

"I cry alone," she whispered to me as I drove on the interminable ride back to her recently downsized modular home stuffed with her oversized furniture and personality.

I never heard her bemoan her fatal fate nor caught a glimpse of self-pity. She wore full force make-up and colorful clothes every day she had remaining. She planted perennials, and boasted to me, "This death sentence means bye-bye budget. I can buy two lipsticks at once if I want."

We shopped for shoes and I bought her a pair of blue suede Ugg boots. It was a tough sell. I wanted her to wear something comfortable and easy to pull on and off. She was distressed that she could no longer wear high heels. My dad had convinced her, "a woman's legs look best in high heels. They call them UGGs because they are UGGly!"

"I don't want to become dowdy," she'd tell me. But as she became more ill, those UGGs felt cozy and warm and became a good memory of a day we spent together. She started to wear them all the time.

One morning I awoke to a frantic call, "I am dying, come get me, and take me to the emergency room." I rushed over to find her waiting in her driveway wearing her full-length mink coat over silk pajamas and that pair of blue UGGs. She looked as pale as the paper on her lit cigarette.

"It's a Lucky Strike," she moaned as I helped her into the car. "A Lucky Strike! If that doesn't make me an oxymoron… maybe just a moron."

Her radiologist had failed to explain that the weekly treatments would constipate her. As stoic as she was glib, and armed with a daily morphine patch, she simply thought not going to the bathroom the past two weeks was a time saving bonus.

The emergency room physician sent her immediately into surgery for fecal impaction.

"You are not the first to tell me I am full of shit," she told the surgeon before they put her under to remove eight pounds of waste.

Sitting with her in the hospital room hours later she told me she had asked to see what was removed from her bowels.

"What?" I replied, aghast by the request, "Why in the world would you want to see… why for gawds sake would you want to look at, I mean…geezus, Mother!"

"It had a little face," she continued, "It even had little hairs."

Now past disgust, I was wincing.

"I named it Joey."

At that, my head snapped toward her. Our eyes locked and in an instant all the absurdities of life, death, cancer, mothers and daughters, indignities, triumphs, legacies, and loss reached a crescendo as we broke into raucous, cleansing, and healing laughter.

From that day on we named anyone rude to us a "Joey." We joked constantly that the whole damn cancer and everything that came with it was a ginormous pile of "Joey."

A day could be a "Joey."

Within six months, my mother was dead. The cancer had spread throughout her body, into her spine and brain, bypassing only her funny bone. I kept the UGGs and have them in my closet; I see them and in my memory, her, almost every day.

None of us can know what will get us in the end. It will be a Joey of some kind. I can only hope when my time comes, I can honor what my mother taught me; be flush with humor, give pain a waggish name, and that it's not enough to die with your boots on…try to leave the legacy of a good laugh.

Put Yourself in My Shoes
Grief doesn't go away,
it walks with you
step-by-step.
RB

We all have had one or more pair of ugly shoes. We all have worn them. They hurt our feet. They don't fit right. They don't fit our look. But over time we wear them in, pair them with some cute outfit or socks and they become a little easier to look at, less hard to accept and wear, more familiar and comfortable. So it is, too, with grief. It's uncomfortable and ugly when you first put it on. There are bumps and it will rub a blister that leaves you limping and feeling raw. No matter what your grief looks like or what you do with it, it's still ugly.

In *The Year of Magical Thinking*, her memoir about grief, Joan Didion writes about giving away her husband's clothing after he has died. She goes into his closet and folds piles of the shirts he wore on their early morning walks through Central Park, bundles them up, and takes them to the Episcopal church across the street. She opens another closet and collects socks and shorts in bags. She returns for his shoes, but she cannot quite bring herself to give the rest of them away. "I stood there for a moment, then realized why: he would need shoes if he was to return."

I think that is why I'm so reluctant to give up my mother's UGGs. If I give away her shoes, I'm severing a final emotional link to her life. And if I lose that link, it's like I further lose her. Pain is real. Pain lives on. I can feel it when I see the shoes, imagine her in them, or write about her passing.

Grief is a dance in uncomfortable shoes; we hear the music, we feel the need to move with it, but sometimes we are clumsy, we lose balance, and we fall. And sometimes we glide gracefully, with ease.

The dance of your grief will sometimes feel like you are doing the twist, or the Lindy or some disjointed movement that makes absolutely no sense. When the relationship to the grief shifts, the dance is smoother, and transforms the grief into grace.

Just know…that it is also OK to wear or keep grief filled shoes for as long as you need them. The dance of grief has no beginning, middle, or end. It's OK if you stand still in your shoes for a bit and sway, just don't stop listening to the music. Eventually, you will feel like dancing again.

Chapter Fourteen

Pump Me Up

The way you are going to move is quite dictated by your shoes.

—Christian Louboutin

Old cheerleaders never die… they just become aerobics instructors.

By now I am certain you have noticed a common theme emerges regarding my feats in these shoes.

I might not be as world renown as I believed my bronzed baby shoes foretold, but I became 'as famous as a boot is to the earth,' like poet Naomi Shihab says, "more famous than the dress shoe, which is only famous to floors."

I was thwarted in my attempts to become an actress, so I became a sage-on-the-stage professor. I write, produce, direct, and star in a piece of theatre every day in front of a paying audience.

I was told I couldn't sing well enough to have lessons, so I became a singing gorilla. I was belting out tunes in public venues for big money.

I didn't have the wherewithal to travel and see the world, so I entered and won a trip that gave me and my family the opportunity to share adventures abroad.

I lacked the talent, gravitas, or celebrity to host my own TV show, so I became a game show regular.

And finally, I continued to envy and envision any little, or big, girl I knew who was trained in dance. I continued to see myself as a potential Rockette, or maybe even an instructor at the Arthur Murray Dance Studio. Alone in my apartment or house, I cranked tunes and pretended I was a hoofer on Broadway, a Bob Fosse acolyte or Goldie Hawn on *Laugh-In.* I even day-dreamed of going to welding school by day and dancing at clubs at night so I could be like the girl in *Flashdance.*

My dance card remained empty until the day I walked into the Jane Fonda Studio on Ventura Boulevard in Encino, CA and found my dance, lunge, squat, and abs partner.

My dad's Volkswagen dealership had provided a car for Jane's latest movie, *The China Syndrome*. He told me she had a fitness studio a block from their home and that she was the nicest, smartest, most beautiful woman he had ever met. He then highly suggested I should go visit her studio and see if any of her attributes would rub off on me.

A former ballet enthusiast, Fonda had begun practicing aerobics to keep fit after an ankle injury. What started out as her rehab became the phenomenal success of her exercise studios, books, and videos. Fonda not only sparked the aerobics trend of the late 1970s and 1980's, aerobics also launched a fashion craze, with neon spandex, legwarmers, and leotards becoming ubiquitous among health-conscious women.

I was a big haired, headband wearing, leg warming, leotard fancying instant devotee the moment I stepped into the studio. The loud music, the 32-count beat, the kicks, the grapevine, the twists and turns, it was déjà vu, again. Aerobics, when it was all boiled down, was a one hour, no pause, cheer routine. Count me in and gimme the beat!

I started with ten classes a week, then fifteen, then twenty. I was getting high on my own supply of endorphins and adrenalin. With these drugs coursing through me I began to judge and then make snide critiques about the instructors for my own amusement.

'If she looked at the class more than herself, that would be refreshing.'

'Is cleavage a job requirement to teach aerobics?'

'Her timing is off a half beat.'

'Those aren't real.'

I was jealous, no doubt, but I was also a shrewd judge of plastic surgery, if nothing else.

When I wasn't working out, I was home perfecting a move or a routine, readying myself for the day I might meet Jane at the studio and hit her up about becoming an instructor.

One afternoon, I was pulling on my pastel pink wrist bands, walking toward my usual spot on the studio floor, nodding, smiling, generally being Miss Congeniality as others took their place when, it happened. Jane practically grand jeté'd into the dance room and we all squealed and applauded, and I swear there were a few genuflects as she said,

"Welcome everyone. My name is Jane, I will be your instructor this morning. Sorry that your usual instructor couldn't be here, she called in sick."

'Like we don't know who she is' I thought. 'I love her already. I am so happy the other instructor is sick.'

Jane was a consummate fitness instructor; warm, lively, strong, no cleavage, minimal make-up, with the ability to create instant rapport.

'Is there nothing this woman cannot do?' I thought, 'She is who I have been trying to be my whole life.'

That thought led me to my next move. After class, I waited while the other giddy girls said thank you and good-bye and tried to get some Jane radiance shined on them. I waited until Jane walked into her office and got some water, I waited until she went to the bathroom and came back out, I waited, until Jane finally said, "Can I help you?"

I had been mentally rehearsing what I was going to say to her since the class ended. It dawned on me that I might look a little deranged hanging in the back of the studio for an extra twenty minutes, drenched in sweat, and mumbling under my breath.

"Oh! Sorry, Miss Fonda, Jane, if I may call you Jane? My dad gave you a car. You even had a photo taken with him. He loves you."

This was not what I had rehearsed, at all. Car? My dad? I was looking and acting even more disturbed with each word I uttered. I swear she backed up a little bit as I continued to talk.

"What I mean to say is, I would like to teach here, for you, with you? Teach aerobics, I could even sign people in, whatever you need. I am good with people, really, not usually this nervous, he-he, but I know most the routines already, I've taken all the classes so many times, I could start today." I was talking fast and had to stop to take a deep breath. I stared at her in wide-eyed awe, which to her probably looked more Charles Manson-ish.

"What do you mean your dad gave me a car?" she asked.

After clearing up her rightful fear that I was a looney-tune, she asked me why I wanted to teach aerobics.

"It's like being a cheerleader to give others a guaranteed good day and a long and healthy life."

I got the job. I helped create the videos, I danced my heart out to multiple performances a day in red, yellow, blue, pink or, orange high top Reeboks, I made friends, I upped my confidence and, I felt like a dancer.

My parents became concerned because I was spending so much time at the studio, working out up to twenty times a week, and I was losing lots of weight.

"You are losing your breasts!" my mother cried one day. Evidently muscle replaces fat of any kind and I was burning though some of my womanly parts. I thought I looked fit, my mother thought I looked flat.

"Why are you spending so much time working out, there must be other things you could be doing that don't cost you your chest."

"Hey," I replied, brightly, "I want to look as good as Jane Fonda when I am fifty."

"You don't look that good now," my dad chimed in.

I spent hours and money I didn't have buying 45-rpm singles and making cassette tapes of hour-long workout music. I carried a boom box bigger than me from class to class, pumped up tunes like "When You See a Chance" by Steve Winwood, "The Power of Love" by Huey Lewis and the News, or "Working in the Coal Mine" by Devo and danced, jumped, kicked, squatted, sit-upped, sweated, and smiled through it all. At last, I was a dancer, a Twyla Tharp of the gym, a Bob Fosse of YMCAs, a Ginger Rogers of aerobics, and Juliet Prowse of jazzercise.

I watched other teachers, took classes, worked with Jane, got credentialed at the prestigious Aerobics Research Center in Dallas, Texas and I am accredited in everything from step to racewalking, Bollywood Dance, and barre. I chutzpahed my way from novice to network television guest *on 20 Minute Workout, The Richard Simmons Show* and *Bodies in Motion,* and countless other appearances on news programs, talk shows, shopping centers, and business openings.

I opened my own studio in Texas named *Aerobix and Go!* because I didn't have a locker room. So, the name meant aerobics is over, go home. I have taught classes in a former dairy barn in Pennsylvania, during lunch hour at an old basketball gym on a university campus, in the backroom of a tanning salon, at a Girl Scout camp, on football fields and tennis courts, in suburban neighborhoods and high rise rec rooms, on the beach, in my backyard, and in a public television station on a show called RondaRobics.

No matter my job, my title, my degrees, my location or my schedule, I have always managed to teach group fitness classes, usually for free and always for fun. Sometimes, like any love affair, it even cost me.

For example, pairing the life of the mind as a professor, with the life of Jamie Lee Curtis in the movie *Perfect* caused some uncomfortable boundary crossings, but none worse than my introduction to a new faculty at a new university department.

The person introducing me to hundreds of faculty, as the newest member of the department, had the wrong resume when he began.

"Ladies and gentlemen, I am honored to introduce Dr. Ronda Beaman. Ronda has been a Marine Corps officer and Lieutenant Governor of Kentucky."

The audience began to look at me like, "Really?" and the guy didn't hear himself talking until he said, "In addition, she has been awarded the International Marksmanship award."

Finally, flustered, he looked up at me—I was standing right next to him—and said, "Do I have the wrong resume?"

There was nervous laughter from the audience, and he tried to save the faux pas by winging my intro.

"Ladies and Gentlemen, this is Dr. Ronda Beaman, she comes to us from Arizona State University where she was awarded a doctorate in leadership." Papers were being shuffled and he was trying his best to regain ground and demeanor when he added, "In her spare time she is an erotic dancer."

The audience again looked at me and I swear their faces were agreeing that, yes this was possible. More possible than being a Marine or Lt. Governor, for sure.

Being an aerobic dancer, a group fitness instructor, a Boot Camp coach, a spin teacher, a barre instructor, and being involved in many other iterations of movement has never been a weight too heavy to carry or a mile to far too travel. Quite the opposite, being fit and helping others do the same has taken me to exotic places, introduced me to a global community, and provided the fuel for feats and the antidote to defeats.

I was diagnosed with multiple sclerosis when I was forty. Being strong and in shape is the only reason I have weathered this challenge and been able to do so without drugs or even momentary doubt that I would and could wrestle MS to the mat.

I may not have been the tiny dancer I wanted to be when I was a little girl, but finding my own way to be a big girl dancer is ten times more rewarding...with the exception that I never got pointe shoes. I still would like to have a pair of pink ones that are beat up, scuffed, and rag tag from years of use.

What I do have, though, is the recent title of Fitness Idol awarded at a national fitness conference where I competed against instructors half my age who jumped twice as high. They had me on looks, on athleticism, on flexibility, and on air-brushed tans. What did I have on them?

I'm not sure. They were amazing.

I still teach barre and boot camp classes. My face looks a little like the scuffed, well- worn ballet shoes I wanted, my feet hurt when I take my first few steps out of bed, I have at least twenty-five pairs of athletic shoes crowding out my dress up shoes, and my hearing has been negatively affected by blaring dance beats and cheap speakers. I have had sprained ankles, a broken wrist, plantar fasciitis, and tendonitis more times than I can count. Sitting on a pillow for my piriformis syndrome and wearing custom arch supports for my Nikes have taken the place of leotards and leg warmers. These are not complaints or regrets, merely opportunity costs.

Recently, I was diagnosed with coxa saltans.

"Eeks, that doesn't sound good," I said. "What is it?"

"It's better known as dancer's hip" the doctor said.

Dancer's Hip! Dancer's Hip! Me!

At last… a bona fide, diagnosed dancer! When the orthopedic doctor gave me the news he was startled when I smiled, fist pumped, jumped off the exam table and cried, "Thank you!"

And thank you, Jane Fonda for the inspiration and innovation to enjoy each plié, lunge, sit up, and step along the way to a fit life and a life that fits.

Put Yourself in My Shoes
The hardest part off any workout is putting your shoes on to do it.
RB

Working out, going to dance class, taking care of your body, even walking around the block, teaches you, enhances you, and empowers you. First of all, it teaches you to stick to things and to work toward improving your lot in life. If you want to succeed in being fit, then there's only one way to do so—and that's to go and workout several times a week like clockwork and to put in maximum effort when you do.

If you learn to do that then you learn to stop making excuses and to stop whining when you have a problem. And because you work on improving yourself, that means you can then help others rather than letting your issues affect them. Truly, in order to be supportive and helpful toward others you need to be sorted in your own life first.

At the same time, when you work out and get stronger, this also makes you more confident and more secure in yourself. That means that you can then be the person who is supportive, encouraging, and flattering–rather than the person who is bitter, jealous, and hurtful.

Better yet, when you have some strength it allows you to have a stronger voice and the confidence to back up what you say when necessary. Because I was fit, I never really felt intimidated by other people and I never gave in to peer pressure. I didn't need to smoke, drink, or do drugs to feel cool and grown up, and no one bugged me about it. Strength means you can accomplish your own feats in your own way, and nothing can hold you back or down.

Working out is a brilliant allegory for how to get more out of life—work hard, be persistent, and persevere. Get some bright, bad-ass sneakers and stop binge-watching; get busy binge-doing! Booyah!

Chapter Fifteen

Converse-Ational

It's not about the shoes. It's about what you do in them

—Michael Jordan

If I didn't change my dress and shoes, I stood a better than average chance of being shot.

I was sitting at my table trying to work up an appetite for the four-star complimentary breakfast at Shangri-La. Nothing looked good. Fish balls? Definitely not. Rice porridge? Risky and rich. Carrot cake? I had finally landed in a place where carrot cake is a traditional breakfast food, and I couldn't even indulge because of the teeming butterflies in my stomach.

I settled on some green tea and plain toast.

In just a few hours I would be delivering a speech at the Singapore Family Ministry. Sipping my tea, I tried to gather my thoughts and calm down by reading through the local newspaper, *The Strait-Times.*

Sleeping well the night before a big speech is always a challenge, second only to picking out what to wear. Should I play the game and dress like a little man in a suit? If I do wear a dress, what length? Can I be tragically hip or comically iconoclast? A lot was determined, of course, by the audience. Bankers? Suit. University students? Iconoclast. Women's Book Clubs? Floral dress. In this case, picking the right outfit became a matter of life and death.

In Singapore, at the time, women did not hold many offices or leadership positions and for them to hire a female executive coach as their featured keynote was bold and unprecedented. I was torn between a black pleated maxi-dress with matching black mid-heels and a rather daring but fun choice; a leopard print sheath dress and golden-beige suede high heels.

Being the first female keynote, I wanted to be masterful, but also memorable. Sincere, and surprising. To be me, and more.

Me + more = the leopard dress. To top it all off, literally, rather than pull my country-western, big and blonde permed hair back or up, I opted for full lion mane style, wild, and did I mention big? Like Reba McIntire, Bon Jovi big.

Wearing the leopard dress, big hair, and golden beige suede high heels, I continued to peruse the newspaper as I sipped my breakfast tea. Headlines: "Massive fires in Indonesia." Weather: "Hot and humid." Comics: "Charlie Brown." Closing the paper, a small, bottom, inside corner headline caught my eye. I almost missed it, but flipped the paper back open to read:

"Local Woman Shot and Killed."

According to the story, the woman was wearing a leopard print sweater and curled up under a palm tree for a nap. The police mistook her for the animal and "Ready, Aim, Fired" a shot that killed her on the spot.

I threw the paper down, jumped up from my table, and took the stairs two at a time in heels, thinking it was faster than the elevator. I was back in my room within minutes, throwing the leopard dress aside for the subdued and professional black dress and matching mid-heel shoes. This speech was going to be tough enough without police barging in with guns pulled, hunting the leopard pacing back and forth on the stage in front of the ballroom. I tied my hair back, took a deep breath, gathered my materials, and elevatored to the conference ballroom.

My dress, turns out, wasn't the only thing that needed changing that day in Singapore. The talk was supposed to motivate the audience of high-level business leaders to spend more time with their families instead of working 60-80 hours a week. Secondly, "it would be wonderful if you can convince them to be better fathers."

It didn't occur to me when I agreed that I hadn't done too well convincing my own father to be better.

After painstakingly writing and re-writing the speech, I believed I had a presentation that would not only succeed at making these men better parents, they would be thanking me with a standing ovation for opening their eyes and hearts to what matters most.

John F. Kennedy once said, "The only reason to give a speech is to change the world." This was my guiding goal.

However, upon entering the venue, I was floored that the room was not set up as I had requested, in rows of chairs three across. No tables, just the three chairs with an aisle down the middle. My idea was to take them on an imaginary Flight to Family complete with custom made and embossed Singapore Airlines "Fathers and Families" tickets given to each participant as he entered the room. Official boarding announcements were read by the emcee and visuals of the sky and clouds appeared as we lifted off. Thinking it was a really clever way to draw an analogy about taking their families with them on this trip called life, I would be captain and flight attendant. So cute. So amusing, yet impactful.

So wrong.

Following the boarding announcement, my introduction, delivered by a government muckety-muck, was a litany of facts and feats designed to build credibility. "Dr. Beaman's book has been translated into five languages" ...blah, blah, blah... "her family has been named most creative in America" ...blah, blah. I could see that the men in the room were unimpressed and bored before I had uttered a word. Many of them were looking down at folded hands on the table or picking at the crumbs left from the carrot cake breakfast. I began to underarm itch and sweat. I had already taxied down the runway, it was too late to abort.

I heard the last line of the introduction and I took off.

My energy and enthusiasm hit them full force, the wrong way. Like a slap upside the head. I swear their hair blew back as if they were in a wind tunnel. And I could tell they thought it was a hot wind tunnel. Nary a smile, a glimmer of encouragement, or even sympathy. Just windblown scowls.

'Geez, maybe their kids are better off with these grumps being at work all the time,' I consoled myself.

Instead of my requested simulation airline seating, there were round tables with ten at each table and twenty to thirty tables were scattered throughout the room. It was impossible to "work the room" as there were no aisles or space to maneuver myself forward and into the audience. I made attempts, but each time I got close to one of the seated groups, the men at the table looked like I imagine the leopard woman did when she realized she was going to be shot.

Suffice it to say, I was not killing it. The hour dragged on and each vignette, quote, suggestion, and statistic crashed. As the speech finally came in for a landing and I uttered my final cockpit announcement "Gentlemen, we are not landing, we are taking flight as fathers," all I could see were hundreds of Singapore businessmen stunned into complete silence. They must have felt hi-jacked and held hostage for the hour. Standing with my arms open and outstretched, they left me hanging for a stricken moment or two before anemic applause started at the table closest to me; a pity, puny clap. A few other audience members joined in. The patter of little hands was almost worse than no applause.

The speech was such a disaster and so embarrassing I considered donning the leopard dress that afternoon and taking a nap in the park. Under a palm tree.

Some people laugh when I tell them I'm a professional speaker. They assume at first that I'm some kind of self-help guru or infomercial star. It's not that I strategically planned on becoming a paid talker. After all, I talked most of my life free of charge. It turns out, however, the combination of university professor, fitness trainer, author, and ham = have voice, will travel.

Speaking for hire has taken me around the world, introduced me to different cultures and people, and deepened my outlook on the power of a well-chosen word, idea, and story. It has given me a wider perspective and more versatile wardrobe.

As faculty for the Young Presidents' Organization (YPO) I had the opportunity to speak at many global gatherings and experience one-of-a kind activities.

In Kyoto, I spent three hours in the salon that decorates genuine geishas each day. The wig alone weighed eight pounds, my kimono was vintage brocade and wrapped so tightly it was painfully clear why geisha's take tiny steps. It has nothing to do with the wooden okobo sandals and everything to do with not being able to move. My three shades beyond white painted face and crimson red lacquered lips made my teeth look so yellow that when I finally appeared and smiled, my husband's geisha fantasy and face blanched.

In my Buenos Aires polo boots, I learned how to play "The Sport of Kings" and even made an assist in the match! My instructors were the national Argentinian Polo Team—the whole team! They all looked like Ralph Lauren models. I will never forget them watching me from the sidelines, riding the fine-tuned, highly trained horse, galloping as fast as possible toward the ball, swinging the long stick above my head in a circle, bringing it down to the ground for the strike, and hearing the team yell "Go, RRRRonda, Go" in their rolling R Latin accent and passionate, deep, smoky voices...but I digress.

Wearing juttis—emerald green, embroidered, and gemstone covered slippers—in Mumbai, and sharing the dais with the Dalai Lama has to be my pinnacle experience of public speaking.

The moment I landed and jumped into one of the 55,000 taxis to get to my hotel, I felt a kinship with the Indian people. It's no secret that driving there is much like the country itself: frenetic. On any given day, animals take up much of the streets; drivers honk incessantly; and cars, scooters, and rickshaws wind past each other as though the rules of the road don't apply. It is frenetic and beloved chaos.

There is no reserve, no distance, no doubt they believe in a more affectionate and active response to life and those living it than other cultures do. Not naming names, or countries, but in Mumbai, predators and people coexist within the city limits. Shooting a sleeping leopard, or woman in a leopard sweater, is frowned upon.

As a speaker at any conference, I am given a time slot and there are usually concurrent sessions. This means that there will be speakers down the hall and in other rooms throughout the hotel competing for audience attendance. It was no different here in Mumbai. I was anxious to get my schedule and see what and who I would be up against. I already knew the Lama would be speaking, as well as astronaut Buzz Aldrin; my fingers were crossed that I wouldn't be presenting during their speeches.

I checked into the Taj Mahal Hotel "Namaste," ordered some room service, "Namaste," arranged for a massage, "Namaste," and at last dug into the conference materials.

The greeting "Namaste"—the god within me sees and honors the god within you—is delivered reverently in any and all interactions between people. Upon seeing the speakers' schedule I knew reverently I needed the god within and without and any people in between to get anyone to come to my talk.

I would be presenting at 1:00 p.m., usually the kiss of death because tummies are filled with lunch and jet lag takes hold. Eyes would droop, heads bob, perpendicular napping ensued with the occasional snort and snore.

'OK, not ideal,' I thought, 'but I can turn it up a bit, no problem.'

My topic, Life 2.0 was an irreverent, nostalgic and heartfelt guideline to making the second half of life meaningful, hopeful, and magical. I believed in the message, I felt like I could rally whoever attended and make them glad they did.

Looking closer, though, I discovered what I was up against was more dire than a chicken vindaloo lunch.

In the room to the left of my assigned room would be the Grand Maharaja of Jodhpur speaking on historical India.

'Oh my God, a real Maharaja? Who wouldn't want to hear and see him?' I silently moaned.

Occupying the breakout room to my right would be Mahatma Gandhi's grandson. His topic? His grandfather, of course.

'Dear God, forget the Maharaja, it's Gandhi talking about Gandhi.'

Down the hall? Down the hall was a female sex expert conversing about pleasing your mate.

'Come on, God, cut me a break!'

And, putting hope that anyone might attend my session to bed, the Dalai Lama would be doing a keynote in the ballroom.

'The god within me is going to be all alone in room five.'

I unpacked, laid out my clothes for the next day, poured myself a glass of wine, and mulled over my options. There wasn't much to be done about the schedule, the line-up, or the topic. I came too far to call in sick. It was too late to add the word "ORGASMIC" to my title. I gulped the wine, poured some more, looked at the gray suit and blue heels I was planning to wear and said out loud, "if you can't beat them, might as well join them."

I marched down to the shopping arcade inside the Taj Mahal Hotel and within the hour had purchased an embroidered Phulkari jacket with matching silk pants, as well as the jade green shoes called juttis. I wasn't a local, royalty, a spiritual leader, or even related to one, and I was no sex expert. There would be no audience, but I would come home with a beautiful souvenir. Who needed success when you could have a sari?

As usual, I arrived a bit early for the gig the next day wearing my native clothing. I took a seat in an ornate gold chair just outside the venue. My Phulkari was cream colored and covered with swirling multi-colored flowers of all kinds outlined in gold thread. My shoes twinkled like diamonds and even a slight move of the purple, blue, and copper bangles on my wrists made a musical, wind chime sound.

A group of conference attendees strolled by and asked if they could take a picture of me.

"You look like an Indian Princess!"

I thought about lying and claiming royalty as a ploy to get them to come to my talk.

More people walked by staring and others stopped to ask about my "costume."

By the time I entered room five to give my talk, I was on cloud nine. My photo had been taken, many compliments had been given, my shoes were sparkling, and my mood was lifted. It no longer mattered who attended, I was having fun. Audience or no audience.

With a couple of stragglers who couldn't get into the other jammed rooms, I left the "speaker" me and allowed the "real" me to talk to them. I Namaste-ed! And the wildest thing happened, other people would look in and then enter, a couple here, a couple there; laughter from the audience drew more passersby, tears on the faces of the audience drew even more people in to hear my talk. It became clear that people were leaving the Maharaja, the grandson, the sex talk, (I am sure no one left the Dalai Lama) and it got so crowded in room five that people were sitting at my jutti clad feet in the front of the room.

By the time I got to my conclusion, there was an overflow of bodies straining to see and hear what I had to say. The applause was thundering, hugs and handshakes were shared, and way in the back of the crowd I saw the hot pink turban of the Maharaja!

I received the highest speaker ratings at the conference! Sorry about the bragging, Dalai Lama. The god in me—not the speaker in me, or the mother in me, or the teacher in me—but the essence of me, felt so good and comfortable in my Indian shoes, in my jacket from Mumbai, and in my skin, I could, at last, reach others with authentic, vulnerable, words and thoughts. Finding my voice wasn't about being a different person, it was being a better version of the person I already am.

It took decades, failures, and poor fits, but now my words and my voice, my goals and dreams come from a place far beyond what I look like, who made my shoes, or what my dad thought. I can speak up whether others agree with me or not, and I can listen to their voices with compassion and understanding.

Now my talks, teaching, coaching, or conversations are like a mandala and a mantra. Any good I can do from speaking goes around and comes around from one god within to another. And another, and another. It's a relatively small circle, but if enough people join me, this is how the world can change.

Red Converse sneakers have become my signature shoe. I wear them to many talks, including my most recent TEDx at the Hague in Amsterdam. Like me, the shoes are an unusual choice; not subtle and, at first glance, too casual. But they are also comfortable, bright, and without guile. They do the job with panache and aplomb and allow for some fancy footwork. I run, jump, and twirl. I feel good in them. I am true in them.

No matter what words I use, and without clicking my heels three times, I believe it's finally my authentic voice the audience hears, whispering,

"You've always had the power, my dear. You just had to learn it for yourself."

Every one of us is, in effect, a public speaker. You came here with something to add, something to contribute, something to say that can only be said by you. You will give speeches to motivate a roommate to do dishes, or a child to do homework, or a friend to carry on. Every single idea in the history of the world had to be explained to at least one other person before it got approved, believed, or accepted by anyone else.

And yet.

Most of us are scared by the idea of speaking up, tongue-tied at important moments, and downright lousy at conveying how we feel and what we need. Many of us lose our voice, the essence of who we are; we lose our truth; our sole purpose.

Finding your voice, and owning it, is tough. I know this because I was in your shoes. Whether trying to please parents, win over an audience, be attractive or liked, we're all worried about how the world sees us…and we conform.

This is how we learn how to be boring. This is why we pick the more subtle dress, the plain shoes, or the safest option. This is also how we lose our voice.

Ignoring your voice leads to frustration—a continuing fear of expression. If you ignore or lose your voice you will stumble in achieving goals. It leads to regret. The biggest fallout from losing your voice is not living your fullest life, not saying what you came here to say.

Chapter Sixteen

Act Your Shoe Size, Not your Age

Please send me your last pair of shoes, worn out with dancing as you mentioned in your letter, so that I might have something to press against my heart.

—Johann Wolfgang von Goethe

The most expensive and, as yet, unworn shoes I have are beckoning at the back of a deep, dark closet I dread going in, on a hidden shelf that becomes more visible day by day, hour by hour.

All the shoes I have ever worn, as well as my feats in them, have a life span. So do I. My hide will buckle and scuff, my lining will become wrinkled, and my arches will eventually collapse. The support and strength I showed will fade, as will the memories I carry of the streets and highways I have traveled. No amount of polish and shine will cover the marks from the rugged miles and stormy weather I trudged through, and in the end, when my feet finally fail me, what awaits is a box.

But, no matter how many birthdays or pairs of shoes I continue to accumulate, as the years pass, whatever the fits and feats, the failures and foolishness, I choose to be more than an old woman who lived in shoe. I will not throw myself away or let anyone else do it. I refuse to get boxed in by society's expectations of how a woman of a certain age should act.

In 1981, noted anthropologist Ashley Montagu published a book called *Growing Young*. I found a copy in a used bookstore and was instantly intrigued by the title and more than a little interested in the concept. I was approaching my 40th birthday and thought the concept of growing young was certainly a better deal than what my mother said awaited me, "Wait until you turn sixty, it's like you become invisible."

Montagu's book introduced me to the science of neoteny. He wrote that the truth about the human species is that in body, spirit, feeling, and conduct we are designed to grow and develop in ways that emphasize rather than minimize childhood traits. As Montagu said, "We were never intended to 'grow up' into the kind of adults most of us have become."

What is the joy or purpose of spending most of my life protecting myself from surprises, risks, and setbacks? Why buy stumble-proof shoes and take tiny, tentative steps toward my demise? Life is a Jimmy Choo or Christian Louboutin and most people settle for ill-fitting Crocs or dull colored flats.

I don't want a predictable life, free from surprises. My goal is to keep the flexibility, acceptance, and open mindedness of my original childlike brain.

"The pursuit of truth and beauty is a sphere of activity in which we are permitted to remain children all our lives," said Albert Einstein. Long lifers, research shows, have a "childlike curiosity and a life-long love of learning." People who die in their 50s and 60s have this life trajectory: school, then work, and then leisure…in frumpy shoes. But resilient seniors, those who live well into their 80s and 90s, have combined all three variables throughout their lifetime with a dash of color and flair to boot.

No matter what the number of years or lines on my face connote to others, I want my youth to walk around inside me like a queen. Like Bob Dylan said, "If you're not busy being born, you're busy dying."

With this in mind, I have made a practice of doing something every year that updates my life resume and keeps me sharp, off kilter, or challenged. I throw myself into learning something new with the abandon of a five-year-old and the ambition of a twenty-five-year old.

Adding new styles and steps has taken me to places like Bennington, Vermont in pursuit of an MFA.

"Why in the world do you want to go back for another master's degree when you have a doctorate?" My husband was nonplussed.

"I need to be in a world I don't own, in a room where I am not the speaker, or the teacher," I replied, "I want to meet artists and learn a new skill."

"You already write books."

"But I don't know what I'm doing!"

Bennington College has a prestigious list of writers who attended, people like Donna Tartt, Jonathan Lethem, and Kiran Desai…OK, I had never heard of them, but they are famous in literary circles, of which I imagined becoming a member; if I could run the gauntlet of admissions, essays, GPAs, GREs, and references.

Just being middle aged and applying for a degree of any kind is empowering. And unsettling. When asked the date of my last degree, I considered subtracting ten years, if I got caught, I could say it was a typo. Weeks later I received the mail and learned that I had been accepted. 'Hemingway, Wolfe, and all you other writerly writers, here I come!'

The morning of student orientation, wearing Birkenstocks in deference to the hippie reputation of the school, I was first in line to pick up my student ID and information packet. The thrill of being back in school making me giddy and goofy. A student ID!

I walked into a wood paneled room reeking of literature and liturgies. The gray-haired poet serving as dean welcomed seventy-five of us from around the world and told us how select, how special, how scribey we were. I looked around at my new classmates. Making sure I got a seat front row, center, I affirmed my new fellow writers by glancing to my right and left with a smile, bonding over our specialness. Everyone's eyes were peeled forward, however, hanging on the dean's delivery, which was, I must say, poetic. After additional quotes from writers like Jane Austen and Kurt Vonnegut he said,

"I would like for each of you to tell us your name and where you are from, as well as your concentration for the MFA." My stomach flipped. I knew the tell-me-about-yourself moment was critical to whether classmates would like you or not. My palms got clammy instantly.

'Settle down,' I thought, 'it's not like you're running for cheerleader or homecoming queen.'

Or, maybe it was.

I put on the new, non-prescription black framed glasses I purchased to look more literary and settled into what I knew would be a lengthy process. I caught a glimpse of myself in the classroom window—glasses, hair pulled back, and hippie shoes, I was looking so poetess, so Bennington; so far, so good.

Six students delivered their introductions before me. The first woman to speak was to my far left. She looked straight ahead and mumbled something so faintly, no one, not even the dean standing in front, could have heard her. I craned my neck farther than I thought it would go and strained to catch at least a vowel or syllable. Once more I looked around at my classmates, searching the room for someone, anyone who might say, "I can't hear you."

Not one of the would-be writers said, or even wrote, anything. I looked up imploringly at our poet cum dean, hoping he would interject a well-placed,

"Huh?"

Nothing. He either had supersonic hearing, couldn't care less, or was used to this drill.

The next person did the same faint, breathy, silent film type introduction, and the next and next…until me.

I jumped to my feet and turned around to actually face my fellow writers. You would have thought I pulled an AK-47. To a person they drew back as if about to get blasted. Their eyes widened and lips tightened.

In a chipper, west coast friendly, clear and enthusiastic proclamation I said, "Hello! My name is Ronda and I'm from California." All I was missing was my pom-poms.

Strike one.

"I am thrilled and honored to be here with all of you."

Strike two.

"I am concentrating on creative nonfiction."

Strike three.

I was not an east coast intellectual, I was emotive and I wasn't writing poetry or literature. I was "the other" and the silent, mumbling majority wrote me off.

Passing people on the way to class during the remaining term, I smiled and said hello and not one, not one, returned the greeting. Each day felt like being surrounded by Children of the Corn. All the other students started to look like Stephen King or Edgar Allan Poe to me. I was ostracized at the lunchroom and ignored in classes. I was being emotionally bullied by Eudora Welty wannabes.

Turns out my literary leprosy was simply warm up for my first "workshop." A writer's workshop is a longstanding artistic tradition during which the artist sits in silence while everyone else in the room discusses the work as if the artist, or in my case, writer isn't even there. This would be no stretch, as no one wanted to notice I really was there, anyway.

I looked up being "workshopped" online and found adjectives like "crushing, nightmare, hazing ritual, test of endurance, awful, ugh." There were reports of students drinking before their workshops; students crying in class and after it; in many cases students never looked at their workshopped pieces again. The word brutal is often used.

I thought, 'Bring it. I am ready. This whole experience can't get much worse.'

I was wrong.

In a masochistic maneuver, I dressed up for my workshop and brought Hershey's chocolates to pass out to the other students in my group. Kill them with kindness before they murder me approach.

"Hello everybody! This is my first ever workshop, and I want it to be a sweet experience, so help yourself to some kisses." The students stared at me briefly, unblinkingly, then looked down the table at the faculty member in charge, waiting to see what would happen, I suppose. No one took a piece of candy, then or ever because she did not take one. She looked up from my submitted writing and said slowly and clearly,

"There is so much wrong with this project, I don't know where to begin."

The other students quickly looked down at their notes on my manuscript, not wanting to actually witness the coming massacre until it was their turn to, at the very least, maim the over-friendly, candy pushing quokka in the dress.

The venerable Susan Cheever was having a go at me. Author of many books, daughter of an even more venerable author, she tore into my idea, my word choice, my lack of depth, my format, and my future. I met her opening critique and raised her one.

"Well, I have nowhere to go but up!" I laughed, first and last.

For the next hour Ms. Cheever and the workshop participants attacked. The remarks and comments were always, always personal, no matter how often I was told not to take it personally.

"No one wants to hear about your happy successes, that is uninteresting."

"Have you ever thought of the emotional abuse you endured, or are you purposefully denying it?"

"Would you agree your father was a psychopath?"

"You should write more deeply about the effect family secrets clearly had on you."

The workshop is a strange concept, a bit like locking a group of id-ridden two-year olds in a room with a box of hammers and saying, 'Play nice.' I left feeling some combination of demoralized and uncertain. I staggered back to my room and collapsed on my lumpy, over-used, under-washed dorm mattress and contemplated the excruciating experience and considered what I might have learned. Only this. I now know why so many writers kill themselves.

On another of my annual quests to do something new and challenging, I listened to the Jiminy Cricket on my shoulder saying, "You should be on the stage."

'I know, I know, it leaves in ten minutes.' I imagined replying to my dad.

I secretly believed I might have wimped out on pursuing my destiny by changing my major from drama to broadcasting. I might have lost out on being Sutton Foster. Or at least Carol Channing.

There was only one way to find out. Audition for *Bye, Bye Birdie* at the local repertory theatre. Reading the casting call in the paper, I got that twitchy and excited feeling that comes from confrontation with something I want to do but I am afraid to do. True, my shot at a Broadway career was past me but being a local troupe member would be a nice plum on my life list, as well as provide a small idea of what my life might have been as a working actress. If I could get a part.

A neighbor took a close-up photo of me and I blew that into an 8x10 headshot. The acting bio I wrote listed teaching as a performance art and my speaking gigs as experience in live entertainment. Bennington may not have recognized it, but I have a healthy creative streak in my writing. I was feeling pretty plucky, the head shot looked legit and I had the song "Put On a Happy Face" down pat.

The night of the audition I sat in the lobby with all the other actors in town and was getting more shaken as each person called left the lobby and threw themselves with abandon into being Conrad Birdie or Kim McAfee. As best as I could tell, everyone wanted to be the lead. I could hear muffled music through the walls, operatic voices raised and strained to impress, and could see the flop sweat on each hopeful as one-by-one they were excused and slumped out of the building. I was proud of us. All these drama types willing to give up their evenings, their weekends for months, just to entertain their community, for free. Impressive. Maybe they were all simply applause addicts? Still not sure. But one thing for sure, each person waiting to audition was larger than life, loud and, what's the word, well, dramatic.

My name was finally called, kind of…

"Rhoda."

I sat still.

"Rhoda, are you here?"

I looked around for Rhoda. 'Sheesh, Rhoda…quit stalling and face the music like the rest of us.' I thought.

"RHODA BEAMAN. ARE YOU HERE?"

"Oh! "I twirped. "I am so sorry. You mean me?" I stood up and looked apologetically non-actressy as I continued my fumbled reply. "Ronda, my name is Ronda, you know, like 'Help Me, Ronda'…heh, heh…Beach Boys…the song?"

Not a smile, not a glimmer of friendliness or welcome crossed this woman's face as she crossed out what I assumed was my wrong name from the list. I was starting out with the assistant director thinking I was deaf, or worse, a Beach Boy fan.

I gathered my bag of acting paraphernalia, took a deep breath and followed her into the "audition space." This sounds grand, but the room was a paint peeling from the walls, piano fortified closet. In the front was a small table with three chairs occupied by the director, the assistant who was leading me in, and the choral director. I was sick to my stomach, dry mouthed, and desperately seeking a small sign of approval from total strangers who looked like they had just had dinner at IHOP. Carb puffy, self-satisfied, with drips of gravy or syrup on baggy, faded sweatshirts. Ah, the glamorous life behind the klieg lights.

I dug right in with some script reading and gave it my all—all pizzaz, all energy, "All right," they broke in, "let's hear you sing." Each of them wrote some notes while I pulled out my phone to ready the karaoke version and put on my happy face.

I performed the song, which involved not as much singing perhaps, as illustrating nuance, and emphasis in speaking while being buoyed by an orchestral arrangement. The note taking picked up in pace, I finished with a flourish, and they had scribbled on the clipboard paper and then poof, I was told "thank you for coming in" and given the ole 'Shuffle Off to Buffalo'.

My hands were still shaking as I drove home, there was throbbing in my head as the adrenalin subsided, and I felt like I needed a drink, or maybe something stronger. I felt a warm kinship with Matthew Perry and Robert Downey Jr., only drugs could calm down the performing high.

'How fortunate I have been to avoid weekly auditions and self-esteem sabotage by not being an actress,' I thought. 'Not to mention drug abuse.' This line of thinking I believe is called rationalizing. I didn't have the voice, didn't have the training, didn't have star quality, and didn't have what it takes.

What I did have was a part. I got cast…in a non-speaking role. Not a cute co-ed screaming for Conrad Birdie. Not a mom, or a friend of mom, or anyone who said anything. I was offered the part of the mayor's matronly wife.

I was the comic relief.

My role boiled down to fainting when I met Conrad Birdie, fainting in thirty-four shows night after night and matinees on Sundays. In my costume, wig, and make-up I looked like a cross between Betty White and Phyllis Diller. And when I fainted, I brought the house, and my ostrich feathered hat down. And that was it. A two-hour show with me on stage for less than three minutes, totally mute.

A friend who saw the show said, "I didn't know you could stay quiet that long."

Radio talk show host, ballet barre teacher, racewalking competitor, Icelandic horse trainer, life coaching practice; you name it, I have at least tried it. The point was never to find the next great thing to do. It was the trying that mattered. There were countless escapades for which I lacked talent and temperament. Knitting, in my hands, became a competitive sport. I got so fixated on knit one, pearl one, and counting stitches, my back hurt and my shoulders were up around my ears after fifteen minutes of "relaxing" with my needle and yarn.

I considered the stumbling blocks as merely stepping-stones. Attempting knitting, or acting, or sourdough bread baking or anything, for that matter, is my way to lace up. Like buying new shoes. Once they are on my feet, I want to wear them new places. It's fulfilling to step out in a new pair and trod an unknown road. At the moment I do, life again becomes an adventure. Each new challenge energizes me and combusts creative ideas and ideals I might never have had otherwise.

My sister was prettier than me, my brother was smarter, and my parents were better in every way than all three of us combined, or so they said many times in many ways. What gift I was given is a rechargeable battery and an inexhaustible sense of mortality. And a willingness to make life a mistake making place. Over and over.

I didn't like orthopedic shoes when I was six and I won't like them when I'm sixty. My collected shoes, and the feats in them are constant reminders to make my time on earth matter, to take chances, and if I'm gonna stumble, I'm gonna drop in fabulous shoes.

I realize my shoes are less memento and more memento mori on the end of my feet, a reminder not of death, but of life.

Pair by pair I collect them as an art form of experiences that remind me that life is fleeting and valuable, visible proof that every step of my life is beautiful and singular and with time, like shoes, I will eventually wear thin, down and, finally, out.

In the back of my closet, in the depths of my psyche, are my end-of-life shoes. In my mind's eye they are bright red patent leather and highly polished. Once I put them on, or better yet, when the cute young orderly at the Piney Mountain Home for the Aged puts them on, I will be able to see my reflection in the shoes. My shoes will say I am not invisible, I am not dead. With every step I will send love through my soles, kissing the earth with my feet, thanking them for doing their job as I walk forward and toward whatever awaits.

Put Yourself in My Shoes
Even a child with normal feet was in love with the world after he had got a new pair of shoes.
—Flannery O'Connor
RB

Perhaps it's time for you to start acting your shoe size, not your age.

We are constantly pursuing happiness, often with mixed results. Yet children appear to have it down to an art—and for the most part they don't need self-help books or therapy. Instead, they look after their wellbeing instinctively, and usually more effectively than so-called grownups. Well, guess what? Those golden seeds of your youth are still inside, maybe lying dormant, but they are there. How can you grow young of heart, mind and spirit, and body?

TELL IT LIKE IT IS

What does a child do when he's sad? He cries. When he's angry? He shouts. Scared? Probably a bit of both. What we need to do is find a way to acknowledge and express what we feel appropriately, and then— again, like children—move on.

ASK ANYTIME, ANYPLACE

When one of my grandsons needs help with a school paper or finding his tennis racquet, he just asks. He doesn't worry about whether it's convenient or whether he's being a burden, because he's secure in the knowledge that I love him and am willing to help at any time. Why should we expect less of our relationships once we reach adulthood? We may not require the same kind of parental care, but everyone needs help once in a while, whether it's a lift when the car breaks down or a shoulder to cry on during a difficult time. And if we set aside our pride and ask, not only do we activate the support network that is so vital to our wellbeing, we also free our loved ones to ask us for help when they're in need.

LAUGH OUT LOUD

Have you ever noticed how much children laugh? If we adults could indulge in a bit of silliness and giggling, we would reduce the stress hormones in our bodies, increase good hormones like endorphins, improve blood flow to our hearts, and even have a greater chance of fighting off infection. All of which would, of course, have a positive effect on our happiness levels.

MAKE TIME

The problem with being a grownup is that there's an awful lot of serious stuff to deal with—work, mortgage payments, and figuring out what to cook for dinner. But as adults we also have the luxury of being able to control our own schedules and it's important that we make time to enjoy the things we love. Those things might be social, sporting, creative, or completely random…dancing around the living room, anyone?

LIFE IS SHORT, BUY THE SHOES

When we are old, it will not be the things we did we regret. It will be all the unspent life, the risks we didn't take, and the chances we avoided that will haunt us. You begin to grow old the moment you say "No" to a new adventure, a different food, an unknown destination, or simply a different path. Make it a priority to live a no regrets life, take on the tough stuff, the weird stuff, take on the wild and wooly, and make your story a page turner. What are you waiting for?

Feats…Don't Fail Me Now!

I want to be an ageless classic, like Audrey Hepburn's ballet flats. Therefore, I will try on:

- Not trash talking about age, or freely sharing mine. The age I feel is on my soul, not a calendar. If I don't tell my body how old I am, it won't know
- Continuing to age proof by staying fit and making friends of all ages
- Setting new goals each year and building my life resume
- Believing there is no age limit to a dream
- Remembering that my worst day is someone else's best day
- Use my footprints to illuminate another life…it's not about what you look like or the shoes you wear, it's the person you've become
- Not stuffing my size seven feet into a size five because that's what I used to be
- Wearing white shoes all year if I want to because guess who makes the rules? I do!
- Owning my lines and their story
- Not holding onto old models, or styles
- Letting my heart determine my age, not my feet

Epilogue

Never a Shoe-In

Shoes are the quickest way for women to achieve instant metamorphosis.

—Manolo Blahnik

From the moment the glass slippers appear on her feet, Cinderella stands up for herself, rebels against her wicked stepmother and takes control of her life.

Dorothy follows the yellow brick road in her ruby slippers to find the Wizard of Oz in search of answers but finally realizes she had them all along.

And after Forrest Gump's mother, Jenny, buys him his white running shoes, he's off on a fascinating life. As she says, "You can tell a lot about a person by their shoes- where they goin', where they been".

The little girl sitting by the pool with her daddy who was told her feet were ugly knew she could hide in shoes. She spent many years learning that she would never find healing at the feet of someone who hurt her.

Something of my own being has gone into my shoes. Nothing came easy to me. I was never the clear winner in anything. But I always stepped up, in, or out. The spirit of the child I was, the cheerleader I became, and the woman who believes there are still miles to go—still opportunities for feats—is alive and kicking. Any blisters, bunions, and corns are what it took in finding the perfect pair to, at last, step into myself.

My shoe wall shelves are filled with the colors, styles, models, and mix of materials of my life; each pair a story, a memory. Each shoe, the vehicle for my journey. How could I have ever started without them? And what roads still await?

Like my shoes, I hope to be worn out in beautiful and appreciated use. And, if, as Ram Dass said, "We are all just walking each other back home," I can guarantee I will have just the right shoe for the occasion.

Acknowledgements

There are two things I can never have enough of: good shoes and good friends.

I am the fortunate recipient of unyielding support from the fabulous Barre Babes, long distance love from Carol Lorek, Cindy Pimental, and Caitlin Dooley, and endurance from my Boot Camp Crew.

A special shout out to Alyn Bartick for the encouragement and Alisha Mathur for the edits. This book would still be in a mixed media mess if not for Katie Martin and Tina Miller. Danielle Durante and Dennis Fennessey fortified my progress with flowers; and thinking of my students, past and present, kept me going.

Thank you to Adelaide Publishing for taking me in and Kelly Harris and Sam Toland for giving me cover.

And, forever, for my sons Chase and Sean who keep me on my toes, my husband Paul who loves shoe shopping, my daughters Katy and Katie who model charm and grace, my grandchildren Lander, Kili, Jet, Sydney, and Merrick who will follow in my footsteps and beyond; I give my heart and sole.

Please follow @FeatsInMyShoes on Instagram, directed and designed by Reiva Trio and Heidi Gill, Hannah Gill and Sarah Hitchings, to read shoe stories from around the world and add your own.

Contact the author for book club appearances or speaking engagements, or just to talk about shoes at featsinmyshoes@ gmail.com.

About the Author

Dr. Ronda Beaman has been Chief Creative Officer for the global research and solution firm PEAK Learning, Inc., since 1990. As a national award-winning educator, Dr. Beaman is Clinical Professor of Leadership at The Orfalea School of Business, California Polytechnic University. She is Founder and Executive Director of Dream Makers SLO, a non-profit foundation granting final wishes to financially-challenged, terminally-ill adults, and serves on the Board of Directors for the National Pay It Forward Foundation.

Her national award-winning book, You're Only Young Twice, has been printed in five languages. Her memoir, Little Miss Merit Badge was an Amazon bestseller and was featured at The Golden Globe Awards. Her new book, Seal With a Kiss, is designed to improve skills for beginning readers and is offered at Lindamood-Bell Learning Centers internationally.

Dr. Beaman is an internationally recognized expert on leadership, resilience, fitness, education, and life coaching. She has conducted research in a host of areas, written many academic articles and books, and won numerous awards. She was selected by the Singapore Ministry of the Family as their honored Speaker of the Year and named the first recipient of the National Education Association's "Excellence in the Academy: Art of Teaching" award. She has been selected as a faculty resource for the Young Presidents' Organization (YPO) university in Argentina, Kyoto and India, where she received the highest speaker ratings among 36 elite faculty. She has been featured on major media including CBS and Fox Television, USA Today, and is a national thought leader for American Health Network.

Dr. Beaman presents to groups from 10 to 10,000 and ranging in ages from 5-105 on a broad range of substantive and inspiring topics. She is described by business and government leaders as "an exceptionally original, dynamic, inspiring, and thought-provoking presenter."

Dr. Beaman earned her doctorate in Leadership at Arizona State University. She is also a certified executive coach and personal trainer with multiple credentials from the Aerobic Research Center. Her family was named "America's Most Creative Family" by USA Today and she was recently named SCW National Fitness Idol.